PETERSON
GROUP
WINTER '94
WIEST

D0572206

To the students in my group classes at

California State University

at Fullerton, who helped in refining the

ideas and exercises in this manual.

Manual for
THEORY AND PRACTICE
OF GROUP COUNSELING

THIRD EDITION

Gerald Corey

California State University, Fullerton

Diplomate in Counseling Psychology
American Board of Professional Psychology

Brooks/Cole Publishing Company
Pacific Grove, California

Brooks/Cole Publishing Company
A Division of Wadsworth, Inc.

© 1990, 1985, 1981, by Wadsworth, Inc., Belmont, California 94002. All rights reserved. No part of
this book may be reproduced, stored in a retrieval system, or transcribed in any form or by any means
—electronic, mechanical, photocopying, recording, or otherwise—without the prior written
permission of the publisher, Brooks/Cole Publishing Company, Pacific Grove, California 93950, a
division of Wadsworth, Inc.

Printed in the United States of America

10 9 8 7 6 5 4

Library of Congress Cataloging-in-Publication Data

Corey, Gerald.
    Manual for Theory and practice of group counseling / Gerald Corey.
    — 3rd ed.
        p.   cm.
    ISBN 0-534-10285-9
    1. Group counseling. 2. Small groups. I. Corey, Gerald.   Theory and practice of group
counseling.   II. Title.
BF637.C6C576 1989 <Suppl.>
616.89' 152—dc20
                                                                                        89-7344
                                                                                        CIP

Acquisition Editor: *Claire Verduin*
Production Coordinators: *Phyllis Larimore, Nancy Shammas, Ben Greensfelder*
Cover Design: *Kelly Shoemaker*
Typewriter Composition: *Maxine Westby*

Acknowledgments

I wish to extend my appreciation to my students at California State University at Fullerton, who used the material in this manual in the Practicum in Group Leadership. I have experimented with the exercises and activities in this revised manual for more than 18 years in order to select the material that students find most meaningful.

Let me give special thanks and recognition to the following students, who served as reviewers of the manual: Donna Smaldino, Debbie Soucy, and Michael Safko are students in our program that reviewed this manual and provided many helpful suggestions for improving its practicality for classroom use. I appreciate the comments of a former student and friend, Paul Jacobson, who now is a therapist at St. John's School in White Water, California. As usual, Bill Waller, the manuscript editor, has done a fine job of editing this manual and the accompanying textbook.

Special thanks go to my wife (and colleague and friend), Marianne Schneider Corey, who helped devise many of the exercises and activities. I am also indebted to these close friends and colleagues for inspiration and challenge in developing the material presented: J. Michael Russell, Patrick Callanan, Helga Kennedy, George Williams, and Mary Moline. We regularly co-lead groups and offer workshops, and the exercises that are presented have been applied to many groups. Our frequent conversations about group work and our actual work of leading groups as a team have kept my enthusiasm for groups high.

I invite you to express your ideas and your reactions to both this manual and the textbook, *Theory and Practice of Group Counseling* (third edition), by writing me at Brooks/Cole Publishing Company, 511 Forest Lodge Road, Pacific Grove, California 93950. For your convenience, you can use the tear-out sheets provided at the end of the text and the manual. Your help will be appreciated.

Contents

I

BASIC ELEMENTS OF GROUP PROCESS: AN OVERVIEW

1
Introduction

This manual is designed to accompany *Theory and Practice of Group Counseling* (third edition), by Gerald Corey (Brooks/Cole, 1990). It is intended to help you gain practical experience in the various theoretical approaches to group work and to stimulate you to think about ethical and practical issues that are typically encountered by group leaders.

The design of the manual is based on the assumption that you will learn best by becoming actively involved in the learning process and by *actually experiencing* group concepts and techniques. Reading about them provides a foundation, but this knowledge remains abstract unless you can see how these theories are actually part of the group process.

I hope the material in this manual will aid your own growth. Much of this material consists of things you can think about, experiment with, and do on your own. There are also many exercises that you can practice in small groups, both as a leader and as a member. You'll be provided with opportunities to function in numerous role-playing situations. I encourage you to modify these exercises so that they will become personally meaningful. The material in the "Exercises and Activities" sections includes:

- self-inventories to assess your attitudes about various theories

- open-ended questions for you to explore

- ideas and suggestions for role playing

- techniques for group interaction

- practical problems that occur in groups

- group exercises for experiential practice

- questions for reflection and discussion

- suggestions of things you can do to apply what you are learning in the course to yourself as a person and as a group leader

There is more material in this manual than a given course can thoroughly cover. However, my preference is to provide a wide variety of activities so that you can select the ones that you find most meaningful. This manual helps you focus as you read, personalize the material, and apply it to the practice of group counseling.

How to Use the Manual and the Textbook

Following are some suggestions for getting the maximum value from the textbook and the manual. These suggestions are based on my experience in using the material in classes, and my students have found them helpful:

1. First, I recommend looking over all the contents of the manual to get an overview of the course and the reading program.

2. Before you read and study a chapter in the textbook, read any summary material in the corresponding chapter of the manual, and then look over the questions and exercises, both in the manual and the textbook. For the chapters that deal with theories of group counseling (Part II), complete the manual's corresponding prechapter self-inventory, which is based on the key concepts discussed in the textbook. Completing these self-inventories will help you determine the degree to which you agree or disagree with the concepts of a given theory. Spending a few minutes reviewing these inventories will give you a clearer focus on the chapter you're reading in the textbook.

3. After reading and studying the text chapter, return to the manual and do the following:

   a. If you have just finished a chapter on theory, retake or at least review the prechapter self-inventory to see if your views have changed.

   b. For the theoretical chapters, study the summary chart that briefly describes the theory's view of the developmental stages of a group.

   c. Look over the basic assumptions of the theory and the summary of key concepts.

   d. Select some exercises to do on your own and some that you would be willing to do in your group or class.

4. The manual is designed as a resource to help you eventually create your own theory and style of group leading. Toward this end, I recommend that as you read and study the textbook and manual, you select specific aspects of each approach that appear to be suited to your personality. The manual's main purpose is to make these theories and issues come alive to you. To accomplish this aim it is essential that you involve yourself actively by thinking critically, share your thoughts with others in class, and, if appropriate, invest yourself personally by bringing your own life experience into this course.

5. As you read and study, be alert for topics for class discussion and points that most interest you. Write down a few key questions, and bring them to class. Look for concepts and techniques that you can apply to the group you are leading or expect to be leading. As you work through the material, develop a capacity for critical evaluation by thinking about what you *most like* and *least like* about each of the theories. The charts dealing with the stages of development as applied to each theory are especially useful.

6. It is very helpful to get some actual experience by working in small classroom groups with the concepts and techniques of the various counseling approaches. The more you are willing to become an active learner and participant in your class or group, the more you'll be able to see the possibilities for actually using these techniques as a group leader. I encourage you to use your ingenuity with the exercises that are presented or the ones you create. Think of ways

to apply the concepts and techniques to groups in various settings. As part of my course, the students meet in small experiential groups (which are supervised) to practice being a group member and co-leading a group. They work within the framework of the model they are studying in class, and in this way they get a better idea of how the ten therapies are actually applied.

7. The "Exercises and Activities" include a mixture of discussion questions and personal topics for self-exploration. Here are some cautions and recommendations about using these activities:

   a. The use of the exercises will depend largely on the format of your class. These exercises have been largely designed for use in a supervised group and for classes that include an experiential as well as a didactic component.

   b. Because many of the activities tap into personal material, you will need to decide what you are willing to disclose in your group. It is largely up to you. The purpose of the course is to learn about group process, not to experience group therapy. Yet it is possible to explore some of your personal concerns in a supervised group and at the same time learn how group process works by experiencing a group as a participant. Care should be taken, however, to avoid opening up deeply personal issues that cannot be adequately attended to in an academic environment.

   c. It is essential that certain ground rules be established from the outset, especially rules about level of participation, "right to pass," and matters of confidentiality. The purpose and goals of your class need to be clearly defined and understood. Both your expectations and your instructor's expectations and requirements should be discussed early in the course.

   d. As you study the manual by yourself, you can benefit from reflecting about your personal concerns and by attempting to relate your life experiences to each of the therapies you study. These approaches will have more meaning for you if you apply them to understanding yourself. The manual can help you in this personal application and self-exploration even if you do not have opportunities to participate in a group.

   e. If you take the exercises seriously, your personal problems may come into focus for you. Although this process can lead to growth, it can also involve some anxiety. I hope that you will consider becoming a member of a group (besides any group that might be a part of your course). Through such participation you can explore areas that you want to change, and the experience can provide you with increased empathy for the members of the groups you will lead. My students often mention that their own experience as a client in counseling, especially group counseling, has been the most useful component in actually learning how to facilitate a group.

   f. I present a wide range of exercises that are based on particular therapeutic models. Let me emphasize that strict practitioners of each approach may not use these exercises. My aim is to help you find ways in which to use the concepts of each therapeutic model and to create exercises that you can practice, modify, and adapt to fit your situation. Use these exercises as a basis for creating approaches that will work for your groups.

8. My students generally find it most helpful to keep a journal as a part of their group course. This journal lets them keep track of their experiences as both members and facilitators of groups, and it motivates them to do writing on some of the exercises contained in the manual.

9. Look for opportunities to attend professional workshops and courses that deal not only with group work but also with specialized populations with whom you might work. You will

4

probably find that once you graduate, you will need to keep involved in professional workshops as a way of updating your knowledge, refining your skills, and learning new therapeutic strategies.

10. As a student, consider joining the professional organization of your specialty field. There are many advantages in becoming involved in such organizations, including receiving journals and information about annual conferences and specialized workshops. As a group worker, I recommend that you also join the Association for Specialists in Group Work, ASGW, (a division of the American Association for Counseling and Development). ASGW is located at 5999 Stevenson Avenue, Alexandria, Virginia 22304. As an ASGW student member you qualify for a reduced fee and you receive the *Journal for Specialists in Group Work* four times each year.

2

Ethical and Professional Issues in Group Practice

A Self-Inventory of Your Views on Ethical Practice in Group Work

This inventory is designed to stimulate your thinking about what constitutes ethical practice in the leading of groups. I suggest that you take it before studying the guidelines for group leaders developed by the Association for Specialists in Group Work (ASGW), which follow it. I have students form small groups to compare their reactions to the statements in the inventory. Later in this chapter there are exercises and activities, consisting of case vignettes for you to evaluate, as well as discussion questions pertaining to each of the ASGW's guidelines. These activities provide material for reflection and lively discussion in class.

In taking this first self-inventory, decide for each item the degree to which you think the leader's behavior is proper or improper, using the following code:

1 = This behavior is unethical.

2 = This behavior is somewhat unethical.

3 = I am uncertain about this behavior.

4 = This behavior is somewhat ethical.

5 = This behavior is ethical.

You may have your own reaction to an item besides one of the five listed above. Bring any of your reactions to class to compare with others' ideas.

_____ 1. A leader has no formal training or courses in group work but asserts that the best way to learn how to conduct groups is to do them.

_____ 2. A leader does not screen prospective members, mainly on the ground that members will screen themselves out of a group if they find that it is not appropriate for them.

_____ 3. A counselor continues to lead groups even though claiming to be extremely tired of group work (and not really believing it to be of therapeutic value).

_____ 4. A leader makes tapes of the group sessions without the knowledge and consent of the members, based on the rationale that telling them would inhibit their free participation.

_____ 5. A leader refuses to see members between sessions, even if they request such a private session, and instead asks them to bring up the issue at the next group meeting.

_____ 6. A leader makes it a practice to socialize with members of the group, maintaining that this practice does not inhibit his capacity to work effectively with members.

_____ 7. A leader fails to intervene when several members focus on another member and pressure that person to make a decision.

_____ 8. A leader introduces techniques in a group even though she has not been trained in their use, thinking that this is the best way to learn.

_____ 9. A leader does not discuss with members any personal risks associated with joining a group, on the ground that he should not give members any fears that they might not already have.

_____ 10. A group leader does not mention confidentiality, thinking that if this topic is important, members will eventually bring it up.

_____ 11. A leader consciously attempts to impose her values on group members, based on the assumption that people who attend a group need clear direction from her.

_____ 12. A leader sees nothing wrong in influencing the group in a subtle manner to accept his values.

_____ 13. A leader conducts groups in order to meet personal needs through this work.

_____ 14. A group leader plays favorites and does not strive to treat all members equally.

_____ 15. A group leader fosters the dependence of the members, on the ground that this will enable them to work through early childhood experiences pertaining to dependence/independence struggles.

_____ 16. A leader initiates sexual relationships with certain members, contending that this practice is not harmful because the clients are consenting adults.

_____ 17. A leader allows one member to dominate the group and does not intervene when this member rambles on and monopolizes the group's time.

_____ 18. Without first getting her permission, a leader contacts the parents of an adolescent who has disclosed her dilemma over having an abortion or keeping her child.

_____ 19. A leader is conducting research that involves the group but does not disclose this fact to the members.

_____ 20. A leader is uncomfortable when members explore a conflict, and thus he pushes clients to make decisions too soon.

_____ 21. A leader does not provide any written statements about her qualifications, the purpose of the group, or the procedures to be employed.

_____ 22. A leader does not state what services will be provided within the structure of the group.

_____ 23. A leader allows the expression of pent-up rage in group sessions but does not take precautions to see that members are not physically injured in these exercises.

_____ 24. A leader coerces members to participate in nonverbal touching exercises, thinking that this type of pressure is needed if they are to challenge their inhibitions.

_____ 25. A leader presses members to experience intense emotions and pushes for a catharsis—even if they say they do not want to explore a struggle—out of the conviction that they need to experience their emotions to become free.

_____ 26. A leader frequently brings his outside personal concerns into the group and is willing to be both a member and a leader, on the assumption that such behavior is good modeling.

_____ 27. A leader does not explain a technique that the group will be using and does not give the members a choice whether to participate in this technique.

_____ 28. When confidentiality is broken in a group of high school students, the leader ignores the situation, assuming that to discuss the matter or to take action will make things worse.

_____ 29. A leader forms a group with elementary school children without getting parental permission.

_____ 30. A group leader discusses in some detail her own involvement with drugs, thinking that this will promote openness and trust among a group of adolescents.

ASGW Ethical Guidelines for Group Leaders

Questions to Consider in Examining the Guidelines

This section lists _Ethical Guidelines for Group Leaders_,* which were developed by the Association for Specialists in Group Work in 1980. Following each guideline I raise several questions to help you to critically evaluate it. I suggest that you discuss the issues raised by these standards in small groups in class. As a focus you might think about what guidelines you would suggest changing (or adding or deleting).

1. _Informed consent (Guideline A-1)._ "Group leaders shall fully inform group members, in advance and preferably in writing, of the goals in the group, qualifications of the leader, and procedures to be employed."

   - How can informed consent be handled in both voluntary and mandatory groups?

   - What are some legal and ethical issues pertaining to informed consent?

2. _Screening and orientation of members (Guideline A-2)._ "The group leader shall conduct a pre-group interview with each prospective member for purposes of screening and orientation and, insofar as possible, shall select group members whose needs and goals are compatible with the established goals of the group; who will not impede the group process; and whose well-being will not be jeopardized by the group experience."

   - Is it unethical to fail to screen?

*Reprinted by permission of the American Association for Counseling and Development. Adapted version. See the Appendix for the complete text of the revised ASGW 1989 version of _Ethical Guidelines for Group Counselors_.

- What are some alternatives when screening is not practical?

- How can screening and orientation be handled in mandatory groups?

3. *Confidentiality (Guideline A-3).* "Group leaders shall protect members by defining clearly what confidentiality means, why it is important, and the difficulties involved in enforcement."

  - Under what circumstance must leaders ethically or legally breach confidentiality?

  - How can confidentiality best be taught to group members and maintained?

  - How does confidentiality apply to both voluntary and mandatory groups?

  - How does this guideline apply to minors and their parents?

4. *Scope of services (Guideline A-4).* "Group leaders shall explain, as realistically as possible, exactly what services can and cannot be provided within the particular group structure offered."

  - What are the issues involved in accepting a member who is in individual therapy with another professional?

  - When and how should referrals be made?

5. *Experimental activities (Guideline A-5).* "Group leaders shall provide prospective clients with specific information about any specialized or experimental activities in which they may be expected to participate."

  - How can the scientific rigor needed for quality research be preserved while at the same time respecting the rights of members to be informed about any experimental activities?

  - What are the ethics involved in preparing research reports for an agency or an institution?

6. *Risks involved (Guideline A-6).* "Group leaders shall stress the personal risks involved in any group, especially regarding potential life-changes, and help group members explore their readiness to face these risks."

  - What are some specific ways to reduce potential risks?

  - How can members be told about risks without needlessly agitating them?

7. *Voluntary participation (Guideline A-7).* "Group leaders shall inform members that participation is voluntary and that they may exit from the group at any time."

  - Is it ethical to require group participation?

  - What are the potential problems of allowing members to leave without dealing with the matter in the group?

  - How can we balance "freedom of exit" with commitment to the group?

8. *Recording (Guideline A-8).* "Group leaders shall inform members about recording of sessions and how tapes will be used."

  - What are the purposes for making records?

  - What are the issues to consider when tapes are made?

- What are some ways to ensure confidentiality when audio tapes or video recordings are made?

9. *Coercion and pressure (Guideline B-1)*. "Group leaders shall protect member rights against physical threats, intimidation, coercion, and undue peer pressure."

   - What are the leader's responsibilities to intervene when members attempt to coerce or persuade other members?

   - What are the differences between "undue pressure" and therapeutic pressure?

   - What are some subtle ways in which group members can be pressured?

10. *Imposing leader values (Guideline B-2)*. "Group leaders shall refrain from imposing their own agendas, needs, and values on group members."

    - What are the differences between imposing and exposing leader values?

    - When and under what circumstances is it appropriate for leaders to expose their values in their groups?

    - Is it ever ethical for leaders to "push" certain values?

11. *Use of group resources (Guideline B-3)*. "Group leaders shall insure that each member has the opportunity to utilize group resources and interact within the group by minimizing barriers such as rambling and monopolizing time."

    - Is it the sole responsibility of the leader to make sure that everyone in the group has equal time?

    - How can members best be taught to make full use of the resources available within the group?

12. *Individual treatment (Guideline B-4)*. "Group leaders shall treat each member individually and equally."

    - Should each member be treated "individually and equally" or "individually and fairly?"

    - How might leaders deal with their preferences toward certain members?

13. *Personal relationships (Guideline B-5)*. "Group leaders shall abstain from inappropriate personal relationships with members throughout the duration of the group and any subsequent professional involvement."

    - What constitutes an "inappropriate personal relationship?"

    - What issues are involved when members socialize outside of the group?

    - What are the issues pertaining to social or sexual involvement with members after the termination of a group?

14. *Promoting independence (Guideline B-6)*. "Group leaders shall help promote independence of members from the group in the most efficient period of time."

    - Does this guideline imply that groups should be limited to a specified duration?

- What is the leader's responsibility in fostering independence, and how can this best be brought about?

- What issues are involved when leaders foster dependency as a part of their theoretical orientation?

15. *Use of techniques (Guideline B-7).* "Group leaders shall not attempt any technique unless thoroughly trained in its use or under supervision by an expert familiar with the intervention."

  - What constitutes being "thoroughly trained" in a technique?

  - Should leaders have personal experience (as a member) with any technique they introduce?

16. *Alcohol and drugs (Guideline B-8).* "Group leaders shall not condone the use of alcohol or drugs directly prior to or during group sessions."

  - To what degree should leaders make their policies explicit at the outset?

  - How does this guideline apply to leaders who conduct groups for the rehabilitation of substance abusers?

17. *Goal development (Guideline B-9).* "Group leaders shall make every effort to assist clients in developing their personal goals."

  - To what degree is it essential to establish specific behavioral goals?

  - Does ethical practice entail a contract approach?

18. *Follow-up (Guideline B-10).* "Group leaders shall provide between-session consultation to group members and follow-up after termination of the group, as needed or requested."

  - What are the practical and ethical issues involved in seeing members between sessions on an individual basis?

  - Is it unethical to fail to arrange for follow-up meetings?

  - What are some alternatives to follow-up meetings on either an individual or group basis?

Some Suggestions to Consider for Additional Ethical Guidelines

The following suggested standards are *not* specifically mentioned in the 1980 ASGW's guidelines. Some of them have been added by the ASGW's Ethics Committee for inclusion in the revised 1989 guidelines. What other guidelines would you like to see added?

1. Group counselors stress the importance of confidentiality and must set a norm of confidentiality regarding all group participants' disclosures. The importance of maintaining confidentiality is emphasized before the group begins and at various times in the group. The fact that confidentiality cannot be guaranteed must also be clearly stated.

2. Group leaders might be encouraged to participate as members in a therapeutic group.

3. Group leaders avoid using the group for their own therapy.

4. Group leaders assist members in translating in-group learning to daily life.

5. Group leaders take steps to maintain and upgrade their knowledge and skill competencies.

6. Group leaders become knowledgeable about state laws that affect their practice.

7. In working with minors in a group, leaders first secure written permission from the parents or guardians, except when doing so would not be in the best interests of the minor.

8. Participants in a mandatory group are made aware of any reporting procedures required by the group leader.

9. In involuntary groups every attempt is made to enlist the cooperation of the members and to encourage them to continue on a voluntary basis. It is critical that involuntary members know their rights and responsibilities, including the consequences of failing to participate in the group.

10. Leaders recognize the importance of continuing assessment of their group and assist member in evaluating their progress.

11. Group leaders are aware of the necessity of modifying their techniques to fit the unique needs of various cultural and ethnic groups.

12. Group leaders are aware of their own values and assumptions and how they apply in a multicultural context.

13. Leaders take steps to increase their awareness of how their personal reactions to members might inhibit the group process and they monitor their countertransference.

14. Leaders keep abreast of research findings and developments as applied to groups.

15. If a group is counterproductive for a client, that person should have the right to leave.

16. Members should be made aware of the importance of informing the leader and the group before deciding to leave.

17. Group leaders are able to articulate a theoretical orientation that guides their practice and can provide a rationale for their interventions.

18. Group leaders monitor their behavior and become aware of what they are modeling in the group.

19. Group leaders should not meet personal and professional needs at the expense of the members.

20. Leaders do well to seek out consultation and supervision when they encounter difficulties in a group situation.

Note: At the time this manual was being printed, the ASGW Ethics Committee completed the 1989 revision of "Ethical Guidelines for Group Counselors." The revised version is considerably improved, and many new guidelines have been added. The ASGW Executive Committee approved the revised guidelines on June 1, 1989. See the Appendix (p.153) for a copy of the 1989 revised guidelines. For further information, write to:

> Dr. George Williams, Chair of the ASGW Ethics Committee
> Counseling Department
> California State University, Fullerton
> Fullerton, California 92634

Exercises and Activities

Case Vignettes: Training Group Leaders in Ethical Decision Making

In their article "Training Group Leaders in Ethical Decision Making," Jim Gumaer and Larry Scott describe a survey that they sent to a 20% random sample of ASGW members ($N = 600$) to obtain points of view from experienced practitioners.* The questionnaire asked respondents to rate the *group leader's behavior* in each case according to the following scale: *unethical, somewhat unethical, uncertain, somewhat ethical,* or *ethical.*

Usable responses were received from 122 members across the United States. Of the respondents 56% were women and 44% were men. The age range was 26 to 55. The typical respondent had either a master's degree or a doctorate; worked in a school, a private practice, an agency, or a university; had received didactic instruction in from one to four group-counseling courses; had had a minimum of one supervised group internship; and had had 5 to 15 years of experience. The results of the survey are given in Table 1, following the inventory.

Directions. The following situations in groups are presented for your analysis and for class discussion. Consider these cases in light of the ethical guidelines discussed in the chapter. What do you see as the ethical issues in each situation? To what degree do you think that the group leader in each situation acted in an ethical or an unethical manner? What do you think you would have done differently? How might the situation in each case be remedied? Do you have any thoughts about how an unethical practice might have been avoided? The object of these exercises is to give you practice in ethical decision making and an opportunity to discuss ethical issues involved in the practice of group work. Compare your ratings for these case situations with the ratings by those in the survey, which are presented in Table 1.

Read each of the case situations presented, and respond by placing the number in the blank that best represents your professional ethical opinion regarding the *group leader's behavior.* Use the code of 1 = unethical; 2 = somewhat unethical; 3 = uncertain; 4 = somewhat ethical; and 5 = ethical.

_____ 1. *Informed consent (Guideline A-1).* The group leader assumes that the more information about group process that she provides, the more the members will attempt to please the leader. The leader is opposed to giving prior information in writing or verbally. If members flounder in defining goals, the leader believes that this is part of the group process; therefore, she does not emphasize goal definition. She does not discuss the procedures she will use, because she believes that procedures are not possible without specified goals. Thus, procedures will be dictated by the eventual goals that members define. This leader is convinced that informed consent is not really possible and thinks that members should follow their own spontaneous paths rather than learning about group norms and other expected group behavior.

_____ 2. *Screening and orientation of members (Guideline A-2).* The case involves a busy mental-health clinic that is understaffed. Counselors are under some pressure to do group work as a way of dealing with more clients in a given time. A counselor decides to organize a group by putting a notice on the bulletin board in the clinic and by sending colleagues a memorandum asking for candidates. There are no provisions for individual screening of potential members, no written announcement informing the members of the goals and purposes of the group, and no preparation for incoming members. No information is given to the members about the leader's background, possible techniques to be used, expectations, and so forth. No consideration is given to the leader's qualifications to work with special populations. The receptionist is asked to admit the first 12 people who come to sign up.

---

*"Training Group Leaders in Ethical Decision Making," by J. Gumaer and L. Scott, 1985, *Journal for Specialists in Group Work*, 10(4), pp. 198-204. The inventory presented here is reprinted with permission from the AACD.

The receptionist puts people into the group as they inquire, irrespective of the nature of their problems, and they are simply told to show up at the first meeting.

_____ 3. *Confidentiality (Guideline A-3).* The situation involves a leader who discusses the legal aspects of confidentiality, the reasons for it, and the impact on the group if it is violated. She summarizes member responsibility in keeping confidentiality by saying, "Anything that happens here, stays here." In discussing the importance of confidentiality in the group, she also points out how it can be violated in subtle ways and how confidences are often divulged without malice.

_____ 4. *Scope of services (Guideline A-4).* A group leader, Richard, tells members that he can use hypnosis for a variety of symptoms. When a member asks how extensively Richard has been trained to offer this service, he replies that he has had a 50-hour academic program with some of the leading experts in the field of hypnosis. He neglects to inform the group member that he has had no supervision in the use of this technique. The members take for granted that he is fully qualified to provide this service. During the group sessions he performs hypnosis with seemingly good results.

_____ 5. *Experimental activities (Guideline A-5).* In the initial pregroup screening interview a potential member, Joe, expresses considerable fear about some techniques that he has heard are commonly used in groups. The leader, Alice, immediately conceives of certain procedures that would be beneficial in working through these anxieties. Some of these techniques are experimental and controversial. Alice assumes that if she informs Joe of the details of these techniques, he will choose not to join the group and will be deprived of working through some critical issues in life. Instead of responding to him directly and in detail, therefore, she downplays the nature of the procedures she has in mind and reassures him that this will be a good experience.

_____ 6. *Risks involved (Guideline A-6).* The group is well screened and well prepared in all but a few instances. No attention is given to members' outside relationships and the potential impact of the group on potential life changes. Members are not forewarned about these risks, nor are they helped to explore their readiness to face and deal with those risks that involve lifestyle changes and their family and friends. Members are not told that pain and struggle are often associated with making personal changes. The leader, however, does emphasize the promise of growth.

_____ 7. *Voluntary participation (Guideline A-7).* A leader tells the members: "Because this is a voluntary group, your attendance cannot be required. If at any time you do not want to attend, use your judgment and stay away. If for any reason you find this group is not meeting your needs, you are perfectly free to leave. We want you in this group only if you are choosing to be a member." Several members simply drop out of the group without stating to either the leader or the other members that this is their intention. The leader continues the group, making no references to the missing members.

_____ 8. *Recording (Guideline A-8).* Mary, a group leader, is writing a book on group process. Without informing the members, she makes several recordings of the group to help create good examples for various stages of a group. Her rationale for not telling the members is her concern that if they were informed, the spontaneity of the process would suffer. She takes great care to ensure that no names are used and that the examples are well disguised, and she attempts to protect the members. She informs the editors of what she has done and asks them to pay particular attention to the rights of privacy of the members to ensure that nothing comes out in print that could be associated with individuals in this group.

_____ 9. *Coercion and pressure (Guideline B-1).* Joan is having difficulties with her husband, and she discusses her struggles with him in her group. Before she has really explored this issue and before she has had a chance to express the full range of her feelings and her own part in the conflict, many members intervene with advice, such as "Leave the guy," "You're better off without him," "Don't waste any more of your life—you deserve better," and "If someone did that to me, I sure wouldn't hang around." The leader intervenes and redirects the group discussion to Joan's feelings.

_____ 10. *Imposing leader values (Guideline B-2).* Imagine a group in which several value-laden issues, such as homosexuality, abortion, heavy drug use as part of a lifestyle, and extramarital affairs, have come up for discussion. The leader, Catherine, has definite convictions on most of these issues, but she thinks that to express these values might have an undue influence on the group. Thus, each time she is asked directly about her position, Catherine turns it back on the members by saying, "It seems to be very important for you to know how I stand on this issue. Talk to me about this." She never does state her position on the issues that have surfaced for exploration.

_____ 11. *Use of group resources (Guideline B-3).* A group member, Lucille, is in a constant state of crisis, and most of the group time is used to deal with her troubles. Finally, the leader, Greg, points this out and says, "There seems to be very little time for other group members to explore their concerns." The group immediately confronts Greg with a statement of his insensitivity: "How can you do this to Lucille? Her problems are so much more serious than ours. We are more than willing to give up the time for her."

_____ 12. *Individual treatment (Guideline B-4).* This situation involves a male leader who focuses his attention primarily on several younger women while ignoring most of the other members. He often cuts others short or seems rather impatient when they are working. Eventually, one of the male members confronts the leader on this issue. The leader asserts that the women are much more willing to work than the other members and continues with his selective style.

_____ 13. *Personal relationships (Guideline B-5).* Jack is leading an ongoing group for several months. At times the members have parties, and they inform him that these gatherings have drawn them closer together. They sense a gap with Jack, however, because they see him only in a professional role. They tell him that they miss him at these parties and that it would be good for him and for the group if he came to some of them. They clearly express their desire to get to know him in a more informal situation. Jack decides not to attend.

_____ 14. *Promoting independence (Guideline B-6).* Ken has just finished leading a group that has been meeting weekly for a year. The group expresses a unanimous desire to continue. The members feel good about themselves and one another and are sad to leave these weekly sessions, which they believe have been very productive for them. They express anxiety about continuing to make it without the group support and without Ken's direction. This is the final session, and now they ask him to keep the group going. He decides not to continue the group.

_____ 15. *Use of techniques (Guideline B-7).* Steve, a relatively inexperienced group leader, attends a body-therapy weekend workshop designed to "open the feelings" through use of body-oriented techniques. He is very impressed with the power of these techniques and is eager to try them out in the group he is leading. At the next session of that group one member, Tom, says, "I feel choked up with pain and anger, and I don't know how to deal with my feelings." Steve intervenes by having Tom lie down, and he pushes on Tom's abdomen and encourages him to scream, kick, shout, and release all the feelings he has been keeping pent up.

_____ 16. *Alcohol and drugs (Guideline B-8).* Elizabeth is a group leader who works with adolescents. Jan and Fred typically come to the sessions under the influence of drugs. This is obvious to the others in the group from the two members' fragmented behavior and speech patterns. Thinking that this group might be Jan's and Fred's last chance for making a positive change, Elizabeth hesitates to intervene. She acts as if there were no problem and ignores the behavior.

_____ 17. *Goal development (Guideline B-9)*. Phil begins a group session with this statement, "We are all here, and I assume that you all want something from this group—so let's get down to business right away. Who wants to work?" Because of Phil's skills in working with members, there is rarely a dull session, and things seem to keep moving. He is active in using role-playing techniques, in suggesting homework assignments, in taking members on guided fantasies, and in providing structured exercises. He does not spend group time talking about the members' personal goals or how they might best accomplish what they came to the group to attain.

_____ 18. *Follow-up (Guideline B-10)*. Bill comes to the West Coast from the East to offer a 24-hour overnight marathon group. The group is an intensive one, with many personal conflicts and much emotion. There is no letup in the intensity because Bill assumes that the way to achieve breakthroughs is to "keep at it constantly" so that defenses are broken down. He believes that people develop tough defenses and that the best way to crack them is through a sustained period of confrontations. No follow-up is planned, and he asserts, "Group members are responsible for themselves and will go only as far as they choose." After the marathon ends, Bill leaves the state the next morning to conduct another group.

TABLE 1   Percentages of Response to Case Situations Representing Guidelines of the Association for Specialists in Group Work (N = 122)

Case situations	Unethical	Somewhat unethical	Uncertain	Somewhat ethical	Ethical
A-1, Consent	42	34	3	11	10
A-2, Screening and orientation	84	12	2	2	0
A-3, Confidentiality	0	2	2	5	91
A-4, Scope of services	56	35	2	4	3
A-5, Experimental activities	55	32	6	6	1
A-6, Risks	26	42	11	15	6
A-7, Voluntary participation	19	29	10	12	30
A-8, Recording	84	10	0	5	1
B-1, Coercion	1	1	2	6	90
B-2, Leader values	6	16	16	16	46
B-3, Using resources	0	1	4	7	88
B-4, Individual treatment	78	17	2	1	2
B-5, Personal relationships	0	2	12	8	78
B-6, Promoting independence	0	3	11	12	74
B-7, Techniques	48	30	12	7	3
B-8, Alcohol and drugs	74	16	6	2	2
B-9, Goal development	17	46	16	12	9
B-10, Follow-up	71	20	6	2	1

Note: Percentages have been rounded off to nearest whole percent.

Source: "Training Group Leaders in Ethical Decision Making," by J. Gumaer and L. Scott, 1985, *Journal for Specialists in Group Work*, 10(4), p. 203.

Follow-up Activity

An examination of Table 1 illustrates that even experienced practitioners cannot agree on an ethical course of action in a given situation. The survey data presented indicate that, although trends appear, no clear agreement exists among ASGW members. Once you have had a chance to respond to the case vignettes, a follow-up activity is having a discussion in class to compare responses. This exercise will reinforce the idea that simply knowing ethical guidelines does not ensure ethical practice.

Professional Standards for Training of Group Counselors*

Preamble

Whereas counselors may be able to function effectively with individual clients, they are also required to possess specialized knowledge and skills that render them effective in group counseling. The Association for Specialists in Group Work supports the preparation of group practitioners as part of and in addition to counselor education.

The *Professional Standards for Training of Group Counselors* represent the minimum core of group leader (cognitive and applied) competencies that have been identified by the Association for Specialists in Group Work.

Designated Group Counseling Areas

In order to work as a professional in Group Counseling, an individual must meet and demonstrate minimum competencies in the generic core of group counseling standards. These are applicable to all training programs regardless of level of work or specialty area. In addition to the genetic core competencies (and in order to practice in a specific area of expertise), the individual will be required to meet one or more specialty area standards (school counseling and guidance, student personnel services in higher education, or community/mental health agency counseling).

Directions: Rate yourself on the following competencies, using this scale:

5 = I am especially strong in this competency.
4 = I am very high to good in this competency.
3 = I am just adequate and could surely improve.
2 = I am weak, deficient, and needing much improvement.
1 = I am especially lacking in this competency.

Group Counselor Knowledge Competencies

The qualified group leader has demonstrated knowledge in the following aspects of group work:

_____ 1. Be able to state for at least three major theoretical approaches to group counseling the distinguishing characteristics of each and the commonalities shared by all.

_____ 2. Basic principles of group dynamics and the therapeutic ingredients of groups.

*These *Professional Standards for Training of Group Counselors* (1983) were developed by the Association for Specialists in Group Work. A revised version of these standards (1989) is pending approval by the ASGW Executive Board. The group counselor *knowledge competencies* and *skill competencies* are reprinted by permission of the ASGW. (*Note*: The rating scale is an adaptation of the printed standards, done for the purpose of helping the users of this manual make a self-assessment of their own level of competency as group leaders.)

_____ 3. Personal characteristics of group leaders that have an impact on members; knowledge of personal strengths, weaknesses, biases, and values and their impact on others.

_____ 4. Specific ethical problems and considerations unique to group counseling.

_____ 5. Body of research on group counseling in one's specialty area (school counseling, college student personnel, or community/mental health agency).

_____ 6. Major modes of group work, differentiation among the modes, and the appropriate instances in which each is used (such as group guidance, group counseling, group therapy, human relations training, etc.).

_____ 7. Process components involved in typical stages of a group's development (_i.e.,_ characteristics of group interaction and counselor roles).

_____ 8. Major facilitative and debilitative roles that group members may take.

_____ 9. Advantages and disadvantages of group counseling and the circumstances for which it is indicated or contraindicated.

Group Counselor Skill Competencies

The qualified group leader has shown the following abilities:

_____ 1. To screen and assess readiness levels of prospective clients.

_____ 2. To deliver a clear, concise, and complete definition of group counseling.

_____ 3. To recognize self-defeating behaviors of group members.

_____ 4. To describe and conduct a personally selected group counseling model appropriate to the age and clientele of the group leader's specialty area(s).

_____ 5. To accurately identify nonverbal behavior among group members.

_____ 6. To exhibit appropriate pacing skills involved in stages of a group's development.

_____ 7. To identify and intervene effectively at critical incidents in the group process.

_____ 8. To appropriately work with disruptive group members.

_____ 9. To make use of the major strategies, techniques, and procedures of group counseling.

_____ 10. To provide and use procedures to assist transfer and support of changes by group members in the natural environment.

_____ 11. To use adjunct group structures such as psychological homework (i.e., self-monitoring, contracting).

_____ 12. To use basic group leader interventions such as process comments, empathic responses, self-disclosure, confrontations, etc.

_____ 13. To facilitate therapeutic conditions and forces in group counseling.

_____ 14. To work cooperatively and effectively with a co-leader.

_____ 15. To open and close sessions, and terminate the group process.

_____ 16. To provide follow-up procedures to assist maintenance and support of group members.

_____ 17. To utilize assessment procedures in evaluating effects and contributions of group counseling.

Training in Clinical Practice

Type of Supervised Experience	Minimum Number of Clock Hours Required: Master's or Entry Level Program
1. Critique of group tapes (by self or others)	5
2. Observing group counseling (live or media presentation)	5
3. Participating as a member in a group	15
4. Leading a group with a partner and receiving critical feedback from a supervisor	15
5. Practicum: Leading a group alone, with critical self-analysis of performance; supervisor feedback on tape; and self-analysis	15
6. Fieldwork or internship: Practice as a group leader with on-the-job supervision	25

Evaluating Group-Leadership Competencies

1. Look over your ratings on the 26 *knowledge* and *skill competencies* to get a sense of your current level of proficiency. What do you think you can do to develop those areas where you are weak? Form small groups in class to discuss your self-ratings. As a group, what ideas can you come up with to develop and maintain each of the knowledge and skill competencies?

2. Carefully look at the ASGW's recommendations for *training in clinical practice*. What do you think about the scope of the types of supervised experience (and number of hours for specific experiences) that are suggested? What training in group work have *you* received to date? What supervised group experiences have you had? What experiences do you expect to have by the time you complete your program? Again, form small groups in class, and discuss the ASGW's suggestions and the types of supervised experiences you deem essential. You might also discuss ways in which you can continue to develop group-leadership skills once you complete your program of studies.

3
Group Leadership

Problems and Issues Facing Beginning Group Leaders

The corresponding chapter in the textbook deals with several common problems that group leaders (both those who are beginning and those who are experienced) typically face. Assume that you are now leading or co-leading a group (even though you may not have done so), and give your reactions to each of the following situations. What do you imagine you'd think and feel in each of these cases? Think about your possible courses of action, then discuss these situations in your class/group and exchange ideas. Plenty of role-playing activities can be generated from the material that follows:

1. Imagine yourself getting ready to co-lead your first group. What kind of anxiety would you experience? What would be your main concerns before you actually began the first session? Assume you are meeting your co-leader an hour before the group meets. What things do you think you'd say?

2. Many beginning group leaders are afraid to make mistakes, and out of their fear they may be inactive and may not try interventions or follow their intuitions. How does this description apply to you? Can you think of some ways to challenge yourself and push yourself to be active as a leader? Are you willing to risk making mistakes in doing this? (It would be useful to discuss in small groups how being afraid of making mistakes might result in passive leading and also ways in which you could become more active.)

3. Again in small groups, discuss your thoughts on the topic of leader self-disclosure. How do you decide *what*, *when*, and *how* to disclose in order to make self-disclosure facilitate, rather than interfere with, the group process? Tell others in your group what you are likely to disclose (or not disclose) in a group you are leading, and get their feedback. In your discussion groups work toward developing a brief list of guidelines for appropriate leader disclosure that you can agree on.

4. I believe that it is extremely important for group counselors to be aware of the personal traits and characteristics needed to become an effective leader. Select some of the following questions to discuss in your class or small group, and use them as a basis for self-reflection on effective leadership:

a. Why do you want to lead groups?

b. What do you have to offer as a group counselor?

c. What experiences have you had that you think will contribute to your success?

d. What shortcomings do you have that may limit your effectiveness as a leader?

e. Do you feel a sense of personal power in your own right, or do you depend on a role or position to give you power?

f. In what ways do you appreciate, value, respect, accept, and like yourself?

g. Do you see yourself as having courage? In what ways do you see courage as important for a group leader?

Skills in Opening and Closing Group Sessions

I've observed that leaders in training are frequently ineffective in opening and closing group meetings. For example, I've often seen leaders quickly focus on one group member at the beginning of a session with no mention of the previous session. Members should at least be given a brief opportunity to share what they did in the way of practice outside of the group since the last session. Additionally, I find that it is useful to have each member briefly state what he or she wants from the upcoming session. Closing a group session should entail more than an abrupt announcement of the end of the meeting. It's more productive for the group leader to lead everyone in summarizing, integrating, and helping one another find ways of applying what they've learned in the group to outside situations.

The following phrases, statements, and questions will give you some concrete tools that you can use to develop skills in opening and closing group sessions. Review these lists frequently, and experiment with parts of them at different times. Add your own opening and closing statements to help you get sessions moving well and to end each of your meetings most effectively. I hope you will not employ these phrases mechanically; rather, you should find a way to introduce them in timely and appropriate ways. Eventually, some of these catalytic statements can become a natural part of your own leadership style.

Guidelines for Opening Group Sessions

- What do you want most from today's session?

- Last week we left off with _____.

- Did anyone have any afterthoughts about our last meeting?

- I'd like to share some of my thoughts regarding our last session.

- My expectations and hopes for this session are _____.

- What did you do this week with what you learned in the last session?

- I'd like to go around the group and have each person complete the sentence, "Right now I'm feeling _____."

- How would each of you like to be different today from the way you were last session?

- Let's go around the group and have each person briefly say what your issues or agendas are for this session. What does each of you want from the group today?

- If you do not participate in the group today, how will that be for you?

- Please close your eyes. Realize that the next two hours are set aside for you. Ask yourself what you want and what you are willing to do in the group today.

- How is each of you feeling about being here today?

- What are you willing to do to make this session productive?

- If you're here only because you're required to be, are you still willing to keep yourself open to getting something from the session?

- Today marks the halfway point for our group. We have 10 weeks remaining, and I'd like to discuss whether there is anything you'd like to change during that time. How would each of you like to be different?

- Is there any unfinished business from the last session that anyone wants to pursue?

- I'd like to go around the group and have each person finish the sentence, "Today I could be actively involved in the group by _____."

Guidelines for Closing Group Sessions

- Before we end for today, does anyone want to say something to anyone else in here?

- What, if anything, did you learn in today's session?

- What did you hear yourself or someone else say that seemed especially significant to you?

- If you were to summarize the key themes that we explored today, what would they be?

- What was it like for you to be here today?

- Are there any issues that anyone wants to work on at the next session?

- I'd like to go around the group and have each of you complete the sentence, "One thing I need to practice outside of the group is _____."

- Would each of you finish the sentence, "The thing I liked *best* (or least) about this session was _____."

- Let's spend the last 10 minutes talking about your plans for the coming week. What is each of you willing to do outside of the group?

- A homework assignment I'd like you to consider is _____.

- Are there any changes you'd like to make in the group?

- How is the group going for you so far?

- How much have you contributed to your group so far?

- We had quite an intense session today. I'm wondering if anyone feels "left hanging." Would you like to say how you're feeling now?

22

- Several of you opened up some difficult problems. Although you don't have solutions to those problems, I hope you'll think about the feedback you received.

- Before we close, I'd like to share my own reactions to this session.

- I noticed that you were very quiet during the session. Are you willing to say how this meeting was for you?

- You opened up some pretty scary feelings. You made important steps, and I hope you continue in future sessions with what you're finding out about yourself.

Checklist and Self-Evaluation of Group-Leader Skills

The textbook gives a specific list of 22 group-leader skills. The following form will help you review them and provide you with a self-inventory of your strengths as a group leader and specific areas that need improvement. Read the brief description of each skill, and then rate yourself. Next, think about the questions listed under each skill; these will help you determine your level of skill development and examine your behavior as a leader. Ask yourself which skills you *most* need to develop or improve.

You can profit from this checklist by reviewing it before and after group sessions. If you are working with a co-leader, it could be very useful to have him or her also rate you on each of these skills. These questions can also provide a systematic framework for exploring your level of skill development with fellow students and with your supervisor or instructor.

On these 22 skills, rate yourself on a five-point scale, using this code:

5 = I do this most of the time with a very high degree of competence.

4 = I do this much of the time with a high degree of competence.

3 = I do this sometimes with an adequate degree of competence.

2 = I do this occasionally with a relatively low level of competence.

1 = I rarely demonstrate this or do it with an extremely low level of competence.

You are strongly encouraged to take this self-inventory at three points during the semester or quarter. The three blank spaces to the left of each number are for these ratings. I recommend that you cover your previous ratings with a piece of paper so that you are not influenced by them. It is ideal if you rate yourself (and have your co-leader and supervisor rate you) about every 5 weeks. This will give you a regular pattern of your progress in developing group-leadership skills. Above all, strive for the maximum degree of honesty with yourself as you complete this rating scale and as you reflect on the questions concerning each of these skills.

It is a good idea to circle the letter of the questions that are the most meaningful to you, as well as the questions that indicate a need for further skill development or special attention.

To what degree does the group leader demonstrate the following:

_____ _____ _____ 1. *Active listening*: hearing, understanding, and communicating that one is doing this.
        a. How well do you listen to members?
        b. How attentive are you to nonverbal language?
        c. Are you able to detect incongruity between members' words and their nonverbal cues?
        d. Are you able to hear both direct and subtle messages?

e. Do you teach members how to listen and to respond?

f. Do you focus on content to the extent that you miss how a message is delivered?

2. *Restating*: capturing the essence of what is said in different words with the effect of adding meaning or clarifying meaning.

a. Can you repeat the essence of what others say without becoming mechanical?

b. Do your restatements add meaning to what was said by a member?

c. Do your restatements eliminate ambiguity and give sharper focus to what was said?

d. Do you check with members to determine if they think your restatement was accurate?

3. *Clarifying*: focusing on underlying issues and assisting others to get a clearer picture of what they are thinking or feeling.

a. Do your clarifying remarks help members sort out conflicting feelings?

b. Are you able to focus on underlying issues?

c. Do members get a clearer focus on what they are thinking and feeling?

d. Does your clarification lead to a deeper level of member self-exploration?

4. *Summarizing*: tying together loose ends, identifying common themes, and providing a picture of the directional trends of a group session.

a. Do you use summarizing as a way to give more direction to a session?

b. Do you tie together various themes in a group?

c. Are you able to identify key elements of a session and present them as a summary of the proceedings at the end of a session?

5. *Questioning*: using questions to stimulate thought and action and to avoid a question/answer pattern of interaction between leader and member.

a. Do you avoid overusing questioning as a leadership style?

b. Do you use open-ended questions to encourage deeper exploration of issues?

c. Do your questions lead clients in a definite direction? Do you have a hidden agenda? Do you have an expected answer?

d. Do you model for members a low-level questioning style?

e. Do you avoid bombarding members with questions that set up a question/answer format?

f. Do you ask "what" and "how" questions, or "why" questions?

g. Do you keep yourself hidden as a counselor through questioning instead of making statements?

6. *Interpreting*: explaining the meaning of behavior patterns within the framework of a theoretical system.

a. Can you present your interpretations in a tentative way, as a hunch or a hypothesis?

b. Are your interpretations dogmatic and authoritarian? Do you have a need to convince members of what you see as "truth"?

c. Do you have a tendency to rescue members from difficult feelings too quickly through the use of interpretations?

d. Are you conscious of appropriateness and timing in making interpretations?

e. Do you encourage members to provide their own meaning of their behavior?

f. Do you invite other members to make interpretations?

7. *Confronting*: challenging members in a direct way on discrepancies and in such a manner that they will tend to react nondefensively to confrontation.

a. *How* do you confront members? What are the effects of your confrontations, generally?

b. What kind of model do you provide for confronting others with care and respect?

c. As a result of your confrontations, are members encouraged to look at discrepancies in a nondefensive manner?

d. Do you confront people about their unused strengths?

e. Are you sensitive to the timing and appropriateness of your confrontations?

f. Are your confrontations related to specific behavior rather than being judgmental?

____ ____ ____ 8. *Reflecting feelings*: mirroring what others appear to be feeling without being mechanical.

a. Do you reflect feelings accurately?

b. Do your reflections foster increased contact and involvement?

c. Do your reflections help members clarify what they are feeling?

____ ____ ____ 9. *Supporting*: offering some form of positive reinforcement at appropriate times in such a way that it has a facilitating effect.

a. Do you recognize the progress that members make?

b. Do you build on the strengths and gains made by members?

c. Do you make use of positive reinforcement and encouragement?

d. Does your support allow and encourage members to both express and explore their feelings? Or does your support tend to bolster members and aid them in avoiding intense feelings?

____ ____ ____ 10. *Empathizing*: intuitively sensing the subjective world of others in a group, being able to adopt the frame of reference of others, and communicating this understanding to clients so that they feel understood.

a. Are your life experiences diverse enough to provide a basis for understanding the subjective world of a range of clients?

b. Are you able to demonstrate the ability to adopt the internal frame of reference of the client and communicate to that person that you do keenly understand?

c. Are you able to maintain your separate identity at the same time as you empathize with others?

____ ____ ____ 11. *Facilitating*: helping members clarify their own goals and take the steps to reach them.

a. How much do you encourage member interaction?

b. Do you foster autonomy among the members by assisting them to accept an increasing degree of responsibility for directing their group?

c. Are you successful in teaching members how to focus on themselves?

d. Do you foster the spirit in members to identify and express whatever they are feeling as it relates to the here-and-now process of group interaction?

____ ____ ____ 12. *Initiating*: demonstrating an active stance in intervening in a group at appropriate times.

a. Do you have the skills to get group sessions started in an effective manner?

b. Are you able to initiate new work with others once a given member's work is concluded?

c. Do you take active steps to prevent the group from floundering in unproductive ways?

d. Are you able to get interaction going among members or between yourself and members?

e. Do you avoid initiating to the degree that members assume an active stance?

____ ____ ____ 13. *Goal setting*: being able to work cooperatively with members so that there is an alignment between member goals and leader goals, and being able to assist

members in establishing concrete goals.
  a. Do you help members establish clear and specific goals?
  b. Are you able to help members clarify their own goals?
  c. Do you encourage members to develop contracts and homework assignments as ways of reaching their goals?
  d. Do you impose your goals on the members without making them partners in the goal-selection process?

___ ___ ___ 14. *Evaluating*: appraising the ongoing group process and the individual and group dynamics.
  a. What criteria do you use to assess the progress of your groups?
  b. What kinds of questions do you pose to members to help them evaluate their own gains as well as their contributions to the group?
  c. Do you make a concerted effort to assist members in assessing their progress as a group?
  d. What kind of evaluation instruments, if any, do you think are helpful in assessing the group process?

___ ___ ___ 15. *Giving feedback*: providing information to members in such a way that they can use it to make constructive behavior changes.
  a. Do you continually give concrete and useful feedback to members, and do you encourage members to do this for one another?
  b. Is your feedback both honest and personal?
  c. Do you teach members to sift through feedback and ultimately decide what they will do with this information?
  d. Do you offer feedback that relates to both the strengths and weaknesses of members?
  e. How do members typically react when you give them feedback?

___ ___ ___ 16. *Suggesting*: offering information or possibilities for action that can be used by members in making independent decisions.
  a. Can you differentiate between suggesting and prescribing?
  b. Do you give too many suggestions, and are they just ways of providing quick solutions for every problem a member presents?
  c. Do you rush in too quickly to give advice or information, or do you encourage group members to provide themselves with possible courses of action?
  d. Do you invite others in the group to offer suggestions for members to consider?
  e. Do your directions and suggestions actually restrict members from becoming autonomous?

___ ___ ___ 17. *Protecting*: actively intervening to ensure that members will be safeguarded from unnecessary psychological risks.
  a. Do you take measures to safeguard members from unnecessary risks?
  b. Do you show good judgment in risky situations?
  c. Do you intervene when members are being treated unfairly or are being pressured by others?
  d. Do you talk with members about the possible psychological risks involved in group participation?

___ ___ ___ 18. *Disclosing oneself*: willingly sharing with members any persistent personal reactions that relate to the here-and-now occurrences in the group.
  a. What is your style of self-disclosure? Are you aloof? Do you remain hidden behind a role? Do you model appropriate self-disclosure?
  b. What impact do your self-disclosures tend to have on the group?
  c. Are you willing to reveal your present feelings and thoughts to members when it is appropriate?

_____ _____ _____ 19. *Modeling*: demonstrating to members desired behaviors that can be
practiced both during and between group sessions.
    a. What kind of model are you for your clients?
    b. What specific behaviors and attitudes do you model?
    c. Are you doing in your own life what you ask the members in your group to do?
    d. What might the members of your group know about you by observing your actions in the group?

_____ _____ _____ 20. *Linking*: promoting member-to-member interaction and facilitating
exploration of common themes in a group.
    a. What interventions do you make that enhance interactions between members?
    b. In what ways do you attempt to foster a norm of member-to-member interactions rather than leader-to-member interactions?
    c. What are some specific instances when you would be most inclined to link the work of one member with that of other members?

_____ _____ _____ 21. *Blocking*: being able to intervene effectively, without attacking anyone, when
members engage in counterproductive behaviors.
    a. Do you take active steps to intervene when there are counterproductive forces within a group?
    b. Do you generally block the following behaviors when you are aware of them: scapegoating? group pressure? questioning? storytelling? gossiping?
    c. Do you block counterproductive behavior in a firm yet sensitive manner?

_____ _____ _____ 22. *Terminating*: creating a climate that encourages members to
continue working after sessions.
    a. Do you attempt to get members to transfer what they are learning in the group to their everyday lives?
    b. Do you assist members in reviewing and integrating their experiences?
    c. Do you create a climate in which members are encouraged to continue to think and act after sessions?

Suggestions for Using the Checklist

Obviously, all of the preceding 22 items are not merely skills to learn. Many of them represent attitudes related to your leadership effectiveness; some represent personal characteristics that many writers think are ideal qualities of group leaders. Again, you are encouraged to complete this self-evaluation three times during the course and to use it when you actually lead groups.

Finally, I recommend again that you look over the list and circle the numbers of those items that are most important to you. Then use the following guide to summarize your major strengths, the areas you most need to improve, and the areas that you would like to explore more fully in class. Also, it could be valuable to make comparisons of these ratings; for example, how does your self-rating compare with ratings by your supervisor, your co-leader, and the members of your group?

1. Some areas where I feel particularly strong are: _____

_____

_____

_____

_____

2. Areas that need improvement most are: _____

_____

_____

_____

_____

_____

_____

3. Some specific steps I can take now to work toward improving these skills, attitudes, behaviors, and personal characteristics are: _____

_____

_____

_____

_____

_____

_____

_____

Guidelines for Meeting with Your Co-Leader

In the textbook I make frequent reference to learning to work effectively with a co-leader. If you are working with a co-leader, I cannot overemphasize the value of making the time to meet regularly with him or her before and after group sessions. My students say that, in addition to talking about the progress of members in their group and the progress of the group as a whole, they find it helpful to talk about their relationship with their co-leader. To provide you with some framework for assessing how well you and your co-leader are functioning as a team, I've prepared the following questions. You might look over this list often in your meetings with your co-leader and select those issues that pertain to your relationship at various times. You can identify the areas in which you see yourself functioning especially well and those areas that both of you need to work on improving.

1. Did you select your co-leader, or were the two of you assigned to each other? To what degree is there a trusting relationship between you? Do you respect each other? Are your differences complementary, or do they present problems in your functioning as a therapeutic team?

2. Did the two of you make plans and preparations together as the group was being organized? Are both of you actively involved and interested in the group now?

3. Are you making the time to meet between group sessions on a regular basis? How productive are your meetings? Do you focus exclusively on your group and the members? Or are you also willing to talk about *your* reactions to the group, to the members, and to each other?

4. Are your theoretical orientations compatible? How do your theoretical views affect the goals and procedures of your group?

5. Do you and your co-leader agree on the division of responsibility between the leaders and the members? Are the two of you sharing leadership responsibility to the satisfaction of each of you?

6. Are the two of you together in your expectations of the group?

7. How are the members reacting to each of you as a leader? How are you and your co-leader reacting to each member? Is either of you having particular difficulty with any member?

8. Do both of you feel free to initiate suggestions and techniques in the group? Is either of you "holding back" and hoping that the other will do most of the leading?

9. Are both of you paying attention to how you open the group sessions and how you bring each session to a close?

10. Does each of you think of ways to continually evaluate the progress of individual members and the group as a whole? Do you have some systematic feedback from the members about how they respond to your leadership?

11. Are you in agreement with your co-leader about self-disclosure? Do both of you reveal to the members your reactions to what is going on in the group? If you see things differently from your co-leader, are you open about this in the group? How do you handle problems between the two of you? Are you competitive with each other? Can you talk openly with the members about your relationship and the way you lead together?

12. What is the balance between confrontation and support in your group? Does one of the team typically support the members and the other challenge them? Are both of you able to be appropriately supportive *and* confrontive?

13. How do your two styles of leadership blend, and what effect does your co-leadership have on the group?

14. Do both of you spend time talking about how it is for each of you to lead with the other? Are you able to tell your co-leader what you like and do not like about working as a team?

15. Are the two of you reviewing each session and paying attention to any changes in the direction of the group? Can you profit from any mistakes that you have made? What are you learning about yourselves and about groups by co-leading? Are you devoting some time to making plans for upcoming sessions? And are you able to abandon your plans if it is called for in a particular session?

4

Early Stages in the Development of a Group

Guidelines for Writing a Proposal for a Group

A clear and convincing proposal is often essential for translating a good idea for a group into actual practice. If you are going to create a group under the auspices of your supervisors or an agency, you will probably have to explain your rationale and proposed methods. It is useful to write out your proposal, for doing so can help you conceptualize your goals, procedures, and strategies for evaluation.

The following guidelines provide you with some direction in designing a group. To gain practice in developing, writing, and presenting a proposal, think of a group that you'd eventually like to organize. Once you have decided on a particular type of group (for example, a group for parents who want to learn better child-rearing skills; a group for children in an elementary school; or a group for adolescents who are having problems in school), consider the following questions in drafting your proposal. Later, spend some time in class discussing the various members' proposals and getting feedback from others on how to improve your proposal.

1. What type of group will you create? Will it be a counseling group? a therapy group? a personal-growth group? a consciousness-raising group? long-term or short-term? Will the group have a remedial (treatment) or a developmental (enhancement) focus?

2. Whom is the group for? Is it a particular population, such as children in an elementary school? for outpatients in a community mental-health center? for substance abusers in a residential setting? for parents who are having major problems in relating to their children? for couples who hope to learn better communication skills?

3. What are your goals for this group; that is, what will members gain from participating in the group? What are the short-term goals? Are the goals and objectives specific? How will these goals be accomplished in a group setting? How will the long-range goals of the group be evaluated during the course of the group and once the group comes to an end?

4. Why is there a need for such a group? In what ways would a group provide definite advantages over individual counseling?

5. What are your basic assumptions underlying this project? Do you have a clear and convincing

rationale for your group? Are you able to answer questions that might be raised?

6. Who will lead the group? What are his or her qualifications? If you will be leading the group, will you be doing so alone, or will you be working with a co-leader? What have you learned from doing previous groups that you could apply to the proposed group?

7. What are some of the ways in which you will announce your group and recruit members for it? Where will you get members? What will you want to convey in any written announcements?

8. What kind of screening and selection procedures will be used? What is the rationale for using these particular procedures? Whom will you include, and whom might you exclude?

9. How many members will be in the group? Where will the group meet? How often will it meet? How long will each meeting last? Will new people be allowed to join the group once it has started?

10. What structure will the group have? Will it be designed around special topics and issues? If so, what topics are likely to be the focus of the group?

11. How will members be prepared to derive the maximum benefit from the group? What ground rules will be basic part of the group?

12. Will you ask members to formulate contracts as a basis for structuring the sessions? What are some advantages and disadvantages of using contracts for your particular group?

13. How will you handle the fact that people will be taking some risks by participating in the group? What will you tell them about these risks, and what will you do to safeguard them from unnecessary risks? Will you take any special precautions with minors?

14. Will your group be voluntary or mandatory? If the members are required to attend, what measures are you taking to increase the chances of gaining their cooperation? How might you deal with the resistance of members who do not want to participate?

15. What ethical considerations need to be addressed? Does your proposal reflect an awareness of ethical practice? What ethical guidelines will you follow?

16. What do you expect to be the characteristics of the various stages of the group? What do you see as your function at each of these stages? What expectations do you have for the members at each phase?

17. What techniques and procedures might you employ in the group? Will there be structured exercises? Will you emphasize role playing? Will members be expected to practice new skills outside of the group sessions? What techniques might you use to get members to support one another in their efforts to change, both in the sessions and between meetings?

18. To what extent will you be available for individual consultation with group members? If the members are having difficulties resulting from the group, are you willing to meet with them privately, or do you expect them to bring up these problems in the group? When might you suggest a referral for a particular member?

19. What evaluation procedures do you plan? Will you evaluate each session? If so, how? Once the group ends, what methods might you use to assess the overall effectiveness of the group?

20. What follow-up procedures might you use? Will you meet each member privately to discuss the degree to which he or she has met personal goals? Will you meet with the group as a whole one or more times for evaluation purposes?

Exercises and Activities

Your knowledge of the stages in the development of a group can help you carry out the specific functions of a group leader at these various phases. You can provide needed structure, make appropriate interventions, and predict certain blocks to group process.

Practicing Leadership Skills

The exercises and activities below will give you practice in your class or group in developing the leadership skills needed at each stage. As you read through these activities, select the ones that have the most meaning for you and bring them up in the class/group. You can use some of them on your own as a way of learning techniques for organizing groups, establishing and maintaining a working climate, terminating groups, and opening or closing group sessions.

1. Imagine talking to potential group members. Explain to them what your group is for and how you expect to lead it. Assume that these people have never been in a group before. What would you stress regarding its purposes and procedures?

2. *Screening-interview exercise.* Assume the role of a group leader conducting a screen interview for members of a certain kind of group. Conduct a pregroup interview with a prospective member for about 10 minutes. Then, the one who was interviewed can report on how he or she felt during the interview. What is your interviewing style like? What were some of the most effective questions or interventions? How could the interview have been improved? Next, interview another prospective member so that you can gain from the feedback and try new ideas.

3. *Group member interviews the leader.* Prospective members may want to talk with the leader before they commit themselves to a group. In this exercise the same format can be used as in Exercise 2, except the *group member* (several people in class can volunteer for this role) asks questions of the group leader. This exercise can be done in subgroups so that everyone has a chance to be both the group member and the group leader. Everyone can be invited to make observations and suggestions.

4. Draw up a list of specific questions you as a leader might ask at a screening interview. What would you look for? On what basis would you include and exclude members?

5. How would you turn away a person if you thought either that he or she was not appropriate for the group or that the group was not appropriate for him or her? You might set this up as a group/class exercise. Are you able to not accept a person in a group without conveying rejection?

6. What screening methods, if any, can you apply to involuntary group members? Do you believe that they can benefit? Why or why not? How would you deal with the situation if the agency you worked for insisted that all of the clients attend the group, whether they wanted to or not? Assume that all the mental-health workers there had to use group therapy as the primary treatment method.

7. What would be your rationale for deciding on a homogeneous or a heterogeneous group? Discuss your reasons for your preference. What characteristics would you want group members to have in common?

8. Discuss some of the problems that you might encounter in an open group that you would not be so likely to have in a closed group. How do you expect to deal with the problems that arise in an open group (one with changing membership)?

9. What value, if any, do you see in arranging an initial private interview with each group

member to explore matters such as goals, fears, expectations, questions, and concerns? How would you prepare members of your group?

10. *Initial stages of a group.* Try to recall what it was like for you when you first entered a counseling group *or* any group of strangers. Consider the possibility that your prospective group members feel the same way. Discuss with others in your class/group how you might be a more compassionate leader if you could keep these memories fresh.

11. *Initial-session exercise.* To give you practice in opening a new group, form subgroups of about eight people. Two of you can volunteer to be co-leaders, and the rest are members. The co-leaders' task is to give a brief orientation. Consider some of the following ideas for orienting your group:

   a. Give about a 10-minute *preparation talk* to group members. Tell them the things you'd *most* want them to know so that they could function more effectively as participants throughout the course of the group.

   b. Consider discussing the purpose of the group, the nature of the group as you see it, any ground rules, and any other pertinent information.

   c. Think about telling the members something about yourself. Why are you leading groups? How do you get yourself ready for each group session?

      The members can be given the opportunity to ask questions or to talk about their expectations. After half an hour or so, discuss the exercise. Members can share how they felt during the session and give constructive feedback to the co-leaders.

12. *Trust building.* What are the most crucial tasks during the early stages of a group? Think of the ways in which you would attempt to create trust within the group. Also, think about how you would introduce yourself to your group and how you'd take care of introductions of group members. What are some specific ways in which you might work on building trust at the initial meetings?

13. What are some possible explanations for the conflict that typically occurs in a group's initial developmental stages?

14. Most writers describe conflict, confrontations, competition, rivalry, and jockeying for power as a basic part of a group's evolution. What could you do as a leader to ignore these dynamics? What effect would this choice have on subsequent group development?

15. Assume that you are leading your first group and several members are questioning your level of expertise. How would you deal with this challenge?

16. Imagine that group members are telling you that they see you strictly as "the leader." They ask you to become more like them and to share more of yourself with them. How would you handle this situation? Explain to the group your understanding of the role of group leader.

17. Examine your own patterns of resistance as a group member. List some ways in which you've found yourself resistant in this class/group. Imagine that you are leading a group of people who have many of the same defenses and resistances that you have. How would this be for you?

18. In your own experience as a group member, what has helped you recognize and work through certain resistances? What has hindered you? What might have led you to deeper entrenchment in certain resistances and defensive styles of behaving in a group?

19. Can you respect resistance? Assume that a member says that she doesn't want to press

onward with an issue she's beeen working on. What courses of action would you be inclined to take? Do you see a difference between pressuring members to talk about a given issue and encouraging them to talk about possible fears that keep them from working on the issue?

20. What can a group leader do in general to effectively handle resistances that occur in a group? What are helpful leader behaviors in a group whose members exhibit problem behaviors?

21. Discuss the differences between reducing a person to a label (such as the monopolist, the help-rejecting complainer, the bore, and so on) and describing a specific behavior such as monopolizing. As a group leader, how can you encourage a member to recognize and deal with specific behaviors that are counterproductive to the progress of both the individual and the group?

22. There is a danger of pushing people too soon to give up a defense. Ask yourself if you are able to handle the reaction of a person who relinquishes a defense. For example, if you encourage a member to feel his anger instead of intellectualizing it, could you handle the possible explosive expression of his rage should he experience it fully? How can you determine whether you are competent to deal with what lies under a defense?

23. Your own objectivity can become distorted as a result of countertransference feelings that are aroused in you toward certain clients and that tend to be based on unrecognized and unresolved personal issues. Put yourself into each of the following eight common countertransference situations. How would you fit into each of these situations? What are you aware of in yourself that might prevent you from focusing on the needs and best interests of group members?

   a. You have an inordinate need for reassurance and constant reinforcement; this includes the need to please all the members, to win their respect, to get them to approve of you, and to have them confirm you as a "superb leader."

   b. You see yourself in certain clients; you overidentify with some members to the extent that you take on their problems.

   c. You develop sexual and romantic feelings toward certain members; you engage in seductive behavior and allow your sexual attraction to become a central focus in the group.

   d. You give people advice in such a way that you tell others what to do based on your own needs and values.

   e. You develop social relationships with some members outside of the group and find that you challenge them less during group sessions than you do other members.

   f. You use power over members to prove your adequacy; you gain power through the use of certain highly directive techniques.

   g. You attempt to persuade members to accept the values you hold; you are more interested in having members subscribe to your idea of the right way to live than in letting members decide on their own values.

   h. You see clearly the faults of members and use what they do or don't do to justify poor results in a group; at the same time you are blind to your own shortcomings or your part in the group process.

Helpful Intervention Phrases for the Initial Stage of a Group

A few well-chosen and well-timed words can give group members the guidance that will enable them to explore personal issues in a significant way. My colleagues and I, based on working with groups and training group leaders, have compiled a list of sentences and phrases that leaders can use during the early stage. I hope you will not simply memorize these phrases but will modify them to fit your personal style as well as your specific group population. Although my colleagues and I use many of the following phrases during the initial stage of a group, not all of them are used in a particular group.

- Whom in the group are you most aware of right now?

- How does it feel to be in the room right now?

- Are you here because you want to be?

- What do you most want to get from this group?

- What are you willing to do to get what you say you want?

- Are you willing to try out new things in this group?

- What are three things you want us to know about you?

- If you were to introduce yourself as the person you'd like to be, what would you tell us about yourself?

- What do you know about groups? What expectations are you bringing with you to this group?

- If a friend of yours introduced you to this group, what might he or she say about you?

- What was going on in your life that led you to join this group?

- I hope you push yourself early to get involved. The longer you wait, the more difficult it will get.

- What fears or doubts do you have about this group, if any?

- What do you imagine would happen if you were to disclose the most difficult concern in your life right now?

- What do you fear most? What do you hope for most?

- Why would you want to change anything in your life now?

- What would you most like to say you've learned or decided when you leave the group?

- What you will learn about yourself is largely dependent on your willingness to participate in this group.

- It is important that you express persistent thoughts and feelings.

- If you are in the group now because someone sent you here, how do you feel about that?

Helpful Intervention Phrases for the Transition Stage of a Group

The transition stage is an especially challenging time in a group's evolution. Defenses are typically high, and a leader's interventions need to be carefully made so that resistance is not entrenched. The manner and tone in which a leader phrases his or her interventions is largely responsible for a member's willingness to take risks and to respond to challenges. My co-leaders and I find the following statements and questions to be generally facilitative:

- I notice that you've been very quiet during many of these sessions, and I'd be interested in knowing what it has been like for you to be here and any reactions you may have had.

- The silence in this group doesn't feel good to me. I wonder what is not being said in here that needs to be expressed.

- Are you willing to continue now?

- You say that you're unwilling to continue. What stops you?

- Are you willing to explore the reasons for your reluctance to pursue this topic further?

- What's the worst thing that you can imagine happening if you continue now?

- Whom in this group were you thinking about last week, and what were you thinking?

- If you're experiencing difficulties in this group, I hope you'll be willing to express them and not keep your reactions to yourself.

- Imagine that this is the last chance you have to change your life.

- I'd like to check out with the people in here where we're going as a group.

- Perhaps you'd be willing to tell us some of the ways in which the situation in this group seems like situations you find yourself in outside the group.

- How are you the same person in both the group and daily life?

- I'm having a difficult time with all of the questioning during this session. Would each of you say what's prompting you to ask your questions?

- Rather than giving advice and telling others your solutions to problems, consider saying more about the problems you're struggling with.

- With whom do you have unfinished business?

- If this were the end of the group, would that be all right?

- I'm concerned that you expect change to be easy and that you're looking to me for solutions.

- How would it be for you if you continued the rest of your life the way you are now?

- What are you willing to do with the tension you feel?

- I'm aware that several of you are very hesitant to become involved, and I'd like to talk to you about this.

- I feel as though I'm working too hard at leading and that I'm taking too much responsibility for the outcome of this session. I'd like to explore the balance of responsibility in here.

- So, some of you say you're bored. What's not happening for you in here? What are you willing to do about changing it?

- I feel overwhelmed with the many problems you're presenting. Take a moment to center yourself. If you had to pick just one problem right now, which one would it be?

- You [a monopolizing member] are very willing to talk. I'm concerned that I haven't yet heard from several people, and I'd like to check in with them.

- I'm aware that you're very quiet in this group. Although you say that you learn a great deal by observing others, I'd like to know what it is that you've been observing and how you have been affected by it.

- I know that this conflict is difficult and uncomfortable. I hope you don't give up. We have a better chance to find clarity and understanding if we continue talking.

5

Later Stages in the Development of a Group

Questions for Discussion

1. What are the characteristics that distinguish a group in the working stage from a group that is in transition?

2. How is group cohesion a central variable at the working stage? What factors contribute to this cohesion? If a group you were leading seemed fragmented and lacked any sense of community, what might you say or do? Can you think of some reasons to explain the absence of cohesion?

3. In the chapter, review the therapeutic factors of a group. What are a few of these factors that you think are especially important?

4. Refer to the section of the textbook that deals with the characteristics of an effective working group. What factors do you think are most significant? Discuss your reasons.

5. How would you explain to a group member the nature and purpose of self-disclosure? What are some specific guidelines that are useful in teaching participants the skills involved in appropriate self-disclosure?

6. What is the purpose of confrontation? What would you tell members about doing it in a constructive way?

Assessment Devices for Group Sessions

I present several forms on which members can assess group sessions and one form for leaders. Look over these evaluation forms as examples of assessment devices that you might create for your own groups. As you consider the purpose of your groups, I suggest that you take what you consider to be the best elements of each of these forms and develop a form that will tap the information you are looking for. The first form is one that you can take now to help you answer the question "What kind of group member am I?" The second form consists of 11 items that can be administered in a few minutes at the end of each group session. Tally the results, and if there are any problems apparent, you can bring the matter up for discussion in your group. This form helps chart the results on a weekly basis so that you can see trends in the groups you are leading. The last set of forms are examples of member and leader postsession questionnaires that were developed by Sheldon Rose, Professor of Social Work at the University of Wisconsin (Madison, WI 53706). His forms are reprinted with his permission.

Self-Assessment Scale:
What Kind of Group Member Am I?

I believe that one of the best ways of preparing for effective group leadership is to first become an effective group member. The following self-inventory is geared to help you determine your strengths and weaknesses as a member. I hope you have already had some form of experience as a member of a group. If not, you can rate yourself on the inventory in terms of your behavior in the class you're now in.

After this inventory is completed, the class can break up into small groups; the groups can be composed of people who know one another best. Members of these groups should then assess the self-ratings and discuss how to become a better group member.

Rate yourself on a scale of 1 to 5, with 1 being "almost never true of me" and 5 being "almost always true of me" as a *group member*.

_____ 1. I am an active and contributing group member.

_____ 2. I am willing to raise personal concerns and explore them in the group.

_____ 3. I listen attentively to others, and I respond to them.

_____ 4. I share my perceptions of other members, telling them how I see them and how I am affected by them.

_____ 5. I confront others with care, yet I do so directly.

_____ 6. As a group participant, I not only give direct feedback to others but am also open to feedback from them.

_____ 7. I'm willing to formulate specific goals and contracts.

_____ 8. I'm willing to openly express my feelings about and reactions to what is occurring within the group.

_____ 9. I serve as a positive model to others in the group.

_____ 10. I am active in taking steps to create and maintain trust in the group.

_____ 11. I show that I am willing to put insights into action by practicing what I learn in the group in my life between sessions.

_____ 12. I prepare myself for the group by thinking about what I want from the sessions.

_____ 13. I am willing to get involved in role-playing activities.

_____ 14. I'm able to provide support to others in the group at appropriate times.

Member's Weekly Evaluation of a Group

Directions: The following evaluation sheet can be given at the end of each group session you may be leading. Using such a device will give you a quick index of the level of satisfaction of the members. You can summarize the results and begin a session with the trends that you are noticing from the evaluation sheets.

Have the members circle the appropriate number for each item using the following scale:

1 or 2 = very weak

3 or 4 = moderately weak

5 or 6 = adequate

7 or 8 = moderately strong

9 or 10 = very strong

1. What degree of preparation (reacting, thinking about the topic, reading, and writing) did you do for this week?

   1   2   3   4   5   6   7   8   9   10

2. How would you rate your *involvement* in the group today?

   1   2   3   4   5   6   7   8   9   10

3. How would you rate the group's level of involvement?

   1   2   3   4   5   6   7   8   9   10

4. Rate yourself on the degree to which you saw yourself as willing today *to take risks*, to share with other members what you thought and felt, and to be an active participant.

   1   2   3   4   5   6   7   8   9   10

5. To what degree do you feel satisfied with your experience in the group?

   1   2   3   4   5   6   7   8   9   10

6. To what degree do you feel that the group dealt with issues in a personal and meaningful way (sharing feelings as opposed to intellectual discussion)?

   1   2   3   4   5   6   7   8   9   10

7. To what degree do you experience trust within the group?

   1   2   3   4   5   6   7   8   9   10

8. How would you rate the group leader's level of involvement and investment in today's session?

   1   2   3   4   5   6   7   8   9   10

9. Rate your leader on the dimensions of his or her ability today to create a good working climate as characterized by warmth, respect, support, empathy, and trust.

   1   2   3   4   5   6   7   8   9   10

40

10. A new behavior I tried was _____

_____

11. What I would like to do differently at the next meeting is _____

_____

_____

Member's Postsession Questionnaire*

Please complete the following scales by circling the number that best describes your impressions of yourself in the group, of the group as a whole, and of the leader of the group. When in doubt, circle the number farthest from the center.

In today's session *I* could best be described as

1. understood by others	1	2	3	4	5	6	7	not understood by others
2. understanding others	1	2	3	4	5	6	7	not understanding others
3. incompetent	1	2	3	4	5	6	7	competent
4. independent	1	2	3	4	5	6	7	dependent
5. distant from others	1	2	3	4	5	6	7	close to others
6. sad	1	2	3	4	5	6	7	happy
7. emotional	1	2	3	4	5	6	7	unemotional
8. involved	1	2	3	4	5	6	7	uninvolved
9. unprepared	1	2	3	4	5	6	7	prepared
10. tense	1	2	3	4	5	6	7	relaxed
11. competitive	1	2	3	4	5	6	7	cooperative
12. active	1	2	3	4	5	6	7	passive
13. helpful to others	1	2	3	4	5	6	7	not helpful to others
14. usually angry	1	2	3	4	5	6	7	rarely angry
15. irrational	1	2	3	4	5	6	7	rational
16. moving toward goals	1	2	3	4	5	6	7	moving away from goals

In today's session *the leader* could best be described as

1. understood by others	1	2	3	4	5	6	7	not understood by others
2. understanding others	1	2	3	4	5	6	7	not understanding others

3. competent	1	2	3	4	5	6	7	incompetent
4. distant from others	1	2	3	4	5	6	7	close to others
5. sad	1	2	3	4	5	6	7	happy
6. emotional	1	2	3	4	5	6	7	unemotional
7. confusing	1	2	3	4	5	6	7	clarifying
8. uninvolved	1	2	3	4	5	6	7	involved
9. unprepared	1	2	3	4	5	6	7	prepared
10. tense	1	2	3	4	5	6	7	relaxed
11. cooperative	1	2	3	4	5	6	7	competitive
12. active	1	2	3	4	5	6	7	passive
13. helpful	1	2	3	4	5	6	7	not helpful
14. uninformative	1	2	3	4	5	6	7	informative
15. humorous	1	2	3	4	5	6	7	serious
16. irrational	1	2	3	4	5	6	7	rational
17. concerned	1	2	3	4	5	6	7	unconcerned

In today's session *the group* could best be described as

1. mutually supportive	1	2	3	4	5	6	7	conflicting
2. governed by rules	1	2	3	4	5	6	7	free from rules
3. independent of leader	1	2	3	4	5	6	7	dependent on leader
4. sad	1	2	3	4	5	6	7	happy
5. emotional	1	2	3	4	5	6	7	unemotional
6. satisfied	1	2	3	4	5	6	7	dissatisfied
7. uninvolved	1	2	3	4	5	6	7	involved
8. unprepared	1	2	3	4	5	6	7	prepared
9. tense	1	2	3	4	5	6	7	relaxed
10. important	1	2	3	4	5	6	7	unimportant
11. having fun	1	2	3	4	5	6	7	being bored
12. cooperative	1	2	3	4	5	6	7	competitive
13. helpful to others	1	2	3	4	5	6	7	not helpful

14. cliquish	1 2 3 4 5 6 7	"groupish"
15. irrational	1 2 3 4 5 6 7	rational
16. in constant conflict	1 2 3 4 5 6 7	rarely in conflict
17. off the task	1 2 3 4 5 6 7	on the task
18. attracted to one another	1 2 3 4 5 6 7	unattracted to one another

Leader's Postsession Questionnaire*

Please complete the following scales by circling the number that best describes your impressions of yourself in the group and of the group as a whole. When in doubt, circle the number farthest from the center.

In today's session *I* could best describe myself as

1. understood by others	1 2 3 4 5 6 7	not understood by others
2. understanding others	1 2 3 4 5 6 7	not understanding others
3. competent	1 2 3 4 5 6 7	incompetent
4. irrational	1 2 3 4 5 6 7	rational
5. distant from others	1 2 3 4 5 6 7	close to others
6. sad	1 2 3 4 5 6 7	happy
7. emotional	1 2 3 4 5 6 7	unemotional
8. involved	1 2 3 4 5 6 7	uninvolved
9. organized	1 2 3 4 5 6 7	disorganized
10. tense	1 2 3 4 5 6 7	relaxed
11. cooperative	1 2 3 4 5 6 7	competitive
12. active	1 2 3 4 5 6 7	passive
13. helpful	1 2 3 4 5 6 7	not helpful

During this session *the group* could best be described as

1. mutually supportive	1 2 3 4 5 6 7	conflicting
2. governed by rules	1 2 3 4 5 6 7	free from rules
3. independent of leader	1 2 3 4 5 6 7	dependent on leader
4. sad	1 2 3 4 5 6 7	happy
5. emotional	1 2 3 4 5 6 7	unemotional

6. satisfying	1	2	3	4	5	6	7	unsatisfying
7. uninvolved	1	2	3	4	5	6	7	involved
8. unprepared	1	2	3	4	5	6	7	prepared
9. tense	1	2	3	4	5	6	7	relaxed
10. having fun	1	2	3	4	5	6	7	being bored
11. competitive	1	2	3	4	5	6	7	cooperative
12. helpful	1	2	3	4	5	6	7	not helpful
13. cliquish	1	2	3	4	5	6	7	"groupish"
14. irrational	1	2	3	4	5	6	7	rational
15. in constant conflict	1	2	3	4	5	6	7	rarely in conflict
16. structured	1	2	3	4	5	6	7	unstructured
17. attracted to one another	1	2	3	4	5	6	7	unattracted to one another
18. on the task	1	2	3	4	5	6	7	off the task

*The MEMBER'S POSTSESSION QUESTIONNAIRE and the LEADER'S POSTSESSION QUESTIONNAIRE are derived by Dr. Sheldon Rose, Professor of Social Work, University of Wisconsin. They are reprinted by his permission.

Exercises and Activities

Helpful Intervention Phrases for the Working Stage of a Group

You might find the following sentences and phrases helpful once your group gets under way and people are working. Again, these are not to be used mechanically; rather, they are specific statements that can serve as constructive interventions if you use them in context, with a sense for timing. If you sense that a member is leaving something out, for example, you might intervene with "What are you not saying that needs to be said now?" If these brief interventions are done appropriately, members can be given a gentle impetus to continue. As you lead groups, think of the phrases that are useful to you. Following are some that my co-leaders and I use:

- What would you like to do?

- Do any of you have any thoughts about our last session that you'd like to share?

- What else needs to be said?

- How were you affected by _____?

- How does this issue relate to you? How are you affected by Sharon's work?

- I'd like each person in the group to finish the sentence "_____."

- Could you say what you're feeling or thinking right now?

- I like it when you _____.

- Right now I'm aware of _____.

- Would you be willing to try this experiment to see how it works for you?

- You can cry and talk at the same time. Keep talking.

- Imagine that your mother were here now. What would you want to say to her?

- Don't ask him questions. Tell him how it is for you.

- I notice that _____.

- You say that you're embarrassed by what you revealed. It's important that you look around the room and notice some of the people you're most aware of. What do you imagine they're saying about you now?

- I'm interested in _____.

- I hope you'll consider _____.

- My hunch is _____.

- If your eyes could speak now, what would they say?

- There are tears in your eyes. What are you reacting to?

- What will help you remember what's being said to you?

- You rehearse a lot before you speak. I'd like you to rehearse out loud.

- You experienced a lot of emotions during this session. What did you learn about yourself?

- What decision did you make about yourself in that situation when you were a child?

- You may have told yourself as a child that you had to be that way to survive, but now that decision doesn't seem appropriate.

- Become each part of your dream. Give each part a voice.

- Instead of talking about this situation, live it as though it were happening now.

- If your mother were here, what would you say to her now that you didn't tell her then?

- You have continued indoctrinating yourself with propaganda that you got from your parents. What new sentences could you begin to tell yourself?

- Instead of saying "I can't," say "I won't."

- What can you do between this session and the next to practice what you just learned?

- I think it's important that each of you ask if you're getting what you want from this group and if there are any changes you'd like to see.

- I'd like to review our contracts to determine if any of them need to be revised or updated.

Helpful Intervention Phrases for the Final Stage of a Group

During the consolidation stage of a group it is important for members to think of ways to apply what they've learned in the group to everyday life, to take care of unfinished business, to express their feelings regarding separation, and to make sense of the total group experience. The following phrases and sentences are ones that I frequently use during the ending stage of a group. As you review this list, think of additional statements and questions that would help members accomplish the tasks at this stage.

- What are some of the most important things you've learned about yourself in this group?

- Are there any things you want to say to anyone in here?

- How do you feel about saying good-bye?

- I'm aware of the tendency to forget what we learn in a group, so I'd like to talk about how you can remember what you've learned.

- How can you practice what you've learned here?

- How do you think you'll be different? Don't tell them, show them!

- Whom do you need to talk with outside of the group? What is the essence of what you want them to hear?

- What decisions have you made?

- If we were to meet a year from now as a group, what would you want to say that you had accomplished?

- If you had to say your message in *one sentence*, what would it be?

- Where can you go from here, now that the group is ending?

- How might you discount what you've learned in here?

- What steps will you take to translate your insight into actions?

- I hope each of you will find at least one person in this group to contact if you discover that you aren't putting your plans into action.

- I'd like to spend some time exploring where each of you can go from here, now that our group is ending.

- Let's practice and role-play some of the situations that each of you expects to encounter after you leave the group.

- To what degree did you attain your goals?

- What did it take, and what steps did you go through to get what you wanted out of this group?

- If you are less than satisfied with the outcomes of this group, what contributed to this feeling, and what role, if any, did you play in this outcome?

- If you could repeat this experience, what might you do differently?

- What kept you from becoming closer to others in this group?

- What did you learn about yourself in this group? What did you do to bring this learning about?

- What do you most want to take from this group and apply to your everyday life?

- Don't expect and insist that others in your life be different. If you are different with them, they are more likely to be different with you.

- Remember, when you talk with significant people in your life, the focus needs to be on you.

- What are a few of the most significant things you learned about yourself in this group? How did you learn them?

- The trust and closeness that you are experiencing in this group did not simply happen. You took steps to create this atmosphere. Let's look at what each of you *did* to help create this mood.

6

The Psychoanalytic Approach to Groups

Prechapter Self-Inventories: General Directions

The purpose of the self-inventories is to identify and clarify your attitudes and beliefs about the different theoretical approaches to group therapy. Each of the statements on these inventories is *true* from the perspective of the particular theory in question. You decide the degree to which you agree or disagree with these statements. Complete each self-inventory before you read the corresponding textbook chapter. Respond to each statement, giving the initial response that most clearly identifies how you think or feel. Then, after reading the chapter, look over your responses to see whether you want to modify them in any way. These self-inventories will help you express your views and will prepare you to actively read and think about the ideas you'll encounter in each of the chapters on theory.

I suggest that you go over your completed inventories and mark those items that you would like to discuss; then bring your inventories to class, and compare your positions with the views of others. Such comparisons can stimulate debate and help get the class involved in the topics to be discussed.

Using the following code, write next to each statement the number of the response that most closely reflects your viewpoint:

5 = I *strongly agree* with this statement.

4 = I *agree*, in most respects, with this statement.

3 = I am *undecided* in my opinion about this statement.

2 = I *disagree*, in most respects, with this statement.

1 = I *strongly disagree* with this statement.

Prechapter Self-Inventory for the Psychoanalytic Approach

_____ 1. The key to understanding human behavior is understanding the unconscious.

STAGES OF DEVELOPMENT OF THE PSYCHOANALYTIC GROUP*

Dimension	Initial Stage	Working Stage	Final Stage
Key developmental tasks and goals	Key task is uncovering and exploring unconscious material. Focus is on historical causes of present behavior. Unconscious processes are made conscious by promoting freedom to express any thought, fantasy, and feeling.	The group resembles the original family, allowing members to relive their childhood and get to the roots of their conflicts. Key tasks include recalling of early childhood experiences and reworking of past traumas. The basic work entails recognizing and working through resistances and transferences. Multiple transferences occur in the group; members become aware of past relationships that are brought into the present situation in the group.	Key task is the development of insight into causes of problems. Analysis and interpretation of transference continues. Focus is on the conscious personal action that members can take and on social integration. Main goals are for members to analyze and resolve their own transferences toward other members, and to work through the repetition of behavior from early years.
Role of group leader and tasks	Leader offers support and creates a permissive and nonstructured climate. Leader's tasks include setting limits, interpreting, and getting a sense of the members' character structures and patterns of defense.	Leader makes timely interpretations that lead to insight; helps members deal with anxiety constructively; is aware of countertransference; and helps members deal effectively with resistances and transferences in the group.	Leader relinquishes much of the leadership functions to allow the members a greater degree of independence; guides the members to fuller awareness and social integration.
Role of group members	Members build rapport by reporting dreams and fantasies. They are expected to free-associate with one another's dreams. They are expected to work through resistances that prevent unconscious material from becoming conscious.	Members produce material in a free-floating manner; they ventilate and express feelings over past traumas. Emphasis is on working through transferences with leader and members. Members function as adjunct therapists by saying whatever comes to their mind; they also make interpretations for others.	Resistances and transferences are worked through, and focus is on self-interpretation and on reality testing. Members become able to spot their own transference figures and relationships; they also contribute to the interpretation of the transference of others.

Techniques	Individual sessions are used to create readiness for a group. "Go-around" technique is used as a free-association device, where members respond spontaneously to one another. Initial resistances are dealt with.	Main techniques that are used include free association, interpretation, analysis of resistance and transference, interpretation and analysis of dreams, use of alternate sessions, and use of pregroup and postgroup sessions.	Alternate sessions and the pregroup meeting or postgroup meeting may continue. Attempts are made to help members integrate what they've learned in the group.
Questions to consider	At the first group meeting, how can resistances to joining the group best be dealt with?	How are members relating to others in the group in ways that are similar to how they were in their original family?	During the final stage, how can members be encouraged to take action based on their insight?
	What are some ways that you can use here-and-now material in the group to understand a member's past? How can one's past provide a framework for understanding current behavior?	How can the group be formed so that the recalling of early childhood experiences can best be worked with?	What are some ways of helping members to understand and resolve their transferences to the leader and others in the group?
	What are some ways to encourage members to give unrehearsed reactions to one another?	What are some advantages and disadvantages of the leader's encouraging transference? How can this transference toward the leader be worked with therapeutically?	What are some ways of letting go of the leadership of the group so that the members are encouraged to become increasingly independent?
	What are some values of simply reporting and sharing dreams in a group?	As a leader, how can you utilize the projections of group members? What techniques can you develop to work with projections?	What are some signs that a member is ready to terminate a group?
	How can free association be promoted by the "go-around" technique?	What are some ways to make interpretations of individuals in a group without promoting their dependency on you? How can your interpretations stimulate their searching?	How can alternate sessions promote a degree of independence in the members?
	Are members looking to the leader for direction and cues?		What are some dangers of continuing the group for an indefinite period of time? What are the values of long-term group therapy?
			How can termination best take place in an analytic group?

*The transition stage has been omitted because there are no clear demarcations between these stages. The intent of these tables is to give readers an idea of the early, middle, and ending stages of a group.

Reactions: Summarize your reactions to the psychoanalytic perspective of group developmental stages. What do you like *most? least?* What aspects of this approach would you incorporate in your style of leadership?

_____ 2. In group work it is particularly important to focus on experiences from the first 6 years of life, because the roots of present conflicts usually lie there.

_____ 3. Group work encourages participants to relive significant relationships, and the group ideally functions as symbolic family so that members can work through these early relationships.

_____ 4. Insight, understanding, and working through repressed material should be given primary focus in group therapy.

_____ 5. Free association, dream work, analysis, and interpretation are essential components of effective group work.

_____ 6. Transference should be encouraged in a group, because it is through this process that members come to an understanding of unresolved conflicts in certain relationships.

_____ 7. Because of the reconstructive element of analytic group work, it is best that the process be a long-term one.

_____ 8. An understanding of the forms that resistance takes is essential for the group leader.

_____ 9. Group leaders need to be continuously aware of ways in which their own feelings (countertransference) can affect the group.

_____ 10. The group serves as a mirror for members to see themselves as they are and to get a perspective on how they cope with anxiety in situations outside of the group.

Summary of Basic Assumptions and Key Concepts of the Psychoanalytic Approach to Groups

1. Psychoanalytic therapists pay particular attention to the unconscious and to early childhood as crucial determinants of personality and behavior. Normal personality development is based on a successful resolution of conflicts at various stages of psychosexual development.

2. Psychoanalytic group work focuses on the influence of the past as a determinant of current personality functioning. Experiences during the first 6 years of life are seen as the roots of one's conflicts in the present. Analytic group work focuses on the historical basis of current behavior for the purpose of resolving its persistence in the present. Because it is necessary for clients to relive and reconstruct their past and work through repressed conflicts in order to understand how the unconscious is affecting them now, psychoanalytic group therapy is intensive and generally involves a long-term commitment.

3. The group provides a context for the re-creation of the original family, so that members can work through their unresolved problems. The reaction of members to one another and to the leader are assumed to reveal symbolic clues to the dynamics of their relationships with significant figures from their family of origin. The present reactions of members are traced back and analyzed in terms of past influences.

4. The group context provides opportunities to observe defensive behaviors that were used in childhood. Through feedback individuals can gain awareness of their defensive styles of interaction, and with this awareness they can eventually choose constructive forms of dealing with anxiety.

5. A major portion of group work consists of dealing with resistance, working through transference, experiencing catharsis, developing insight and self-understanding, and learning

the relationship between past experiences and their effect on current development.

6. Analytically oriented group practitioners tend to remain relatively anonymous and encourage group members to project onto them the feelings that they have had toward the significant people in their lives. The analysis and interpretation of transference leads to insight and personality change. (Some analytically oriented therapists do not always remain anonymous, however; they may respond to members in personal ways.) A central task of the leader is to enable members to work through their transference distortions as they become evident in the group.

7. Some of the unique advantages of analytic group therapy are as follows: members reexperience relationships that are similar to their own early family relationships; there are opportunities for multiple transferences; members can gain insight into their defenses and resistances more dramatically than they can in individual therapy; and dependency on the authority of the therapist is lessened because members get feedback from other members.

Exercises and Activities for the Psychoanalytic Approach

Rationale

For the exercises in this section I've selected several group techniques that are based on psychoanalytic concepts and procedures and modified them considerably in the hope that you will be able to apply some of them in your group work. The following exercises are geared to stimulate your thinking on issues such as the value of *working with the past*, being open to what you can learn from the *unconscious*, experimenting with techniques like *free association* and *dream work*, and increasing your appreciation of the importance of central concepts such as *resistance*, *transference*, and *countertransference*. In my opinion, regardless of their theoretical orientation, group practitioners must understand these concepts. As you work through these exercises in your class/group, remain open to ways in which you can incorporate some of them in your style of leading groups.

Since some of these exercises can tap emotional material, it is best to restrict them to a supervised group situation. Some of these exercises may not be appropriate for the format and purpose of your class.

Exercises

1. *Working with your past.* The analytic approach is based on the assumption that past experiences play a vital role in shaping one's current personality. The following short exercises and questions are designed to assist you in remembering and exploring in your group selected dimensions of your past.

   a. Recall and reconstruct some childhood experiences. Examining pictures of yourself as a child, interviewing people who knew you well, looking over diaries, and so on can be useful means of stimulating recall. Share in your group what you consider to be some significant influences from your past. How have these factors contributed to the person you are now?

   b. Write an outline (such as you might find in the table of contents) of a book that you could write about your life. Pay attention mainly to chapter headings. Examples might include: "The child who was never allowed to be a child"; "A time of abandonment"; "My most joyous memories"; "Dreams I had as a child"; "The things I wanted to be as a child." You could also write the Preface to this book about your life and include an acknowledgment section. Who are the people you'd most want to acknowledge as having a significant impact on your life? In what ways have they made a difference?

c. In the outline for the book on your life, include a chapter in which you rewrite your past the way you would have wanted it to be. Share your ideas for this chapter with your group.

d. Make a list of your current struggles, and see if you can trace the origins of these conflicts to childhood events.

e. Freud believed that the events of the first 5 years of life as crucial determinants of our personality. What can you find out about this time in your life? What hunches do you have about the effect of your early years on the person you now are?

2. *Free association.* A key method of unlocking the unconscious is free association; the therapist asks clients to clear their mind of day-to-day thoughts and simply report in a spontaneous way whatever comes to mind. There are several ways to use free association in a group:

a. For example members can be encouraged to say whatever comes to them. Participants often censor their contributions; they rehearse what they will say for fear that "it won't come out right." Some members agonize over what to bring up in a group and exactly how to present a personal issue.

b. It might also be a productive exercise in your group to make up incomplete sentences, finish them, and then find ways to free-associate with what seems to be significant material. For example, you might work with sentences such as:

When I'm in this group, I feel _____.

One way I attempt to avoid things in this group is by _____.

One fear in this group I have is _____.

3. *Dream work.* Report the key elements of one of your dreams to your group. You might try the following suggestions as a way of learning something about yourself through your dreams.

a. Select any part of your dream and free-associate with that part. Say as many words as fast as you can without censoring them. After you've done this, see what your free-association work tells you.

b. Give an initial interpretation of your dream. What themes or patterns do you see?

c. Next, ask group members to give their interpretations of your dream. What do they think your dream means?

d. If they want to, other group members can free-associate with any parts of your dream.

You might want to begin keeping a dream journal. Write down your dreams. Record what you remember. Then look at the patterns of your dreams and interpret their meaning.

4. *Resistance.* Brainstorm all the possible ways in which you might resist in a group. What resistances have you experienced to simply getting into a group? List some avoidance patterns that you have seen in yourself in a group. What are some ways that you can think of to help group members recognize and work through resistances that could prevent them from effectively working in a group? What are some uses of resistances? What purposes do these member resistances serve?

5. *Transference.* A central concept in analytic group therapy is the identification and working

through of transference. To get some idea of this process, try some of these exercises in your group.

a. Think of the people in your group. Does anyone remind you of a significant person in your life? Discuss the similarities.

b. You can explore possible transferences that occur outside of the group. Have you ever experienced strong, immediate, and even irrational reactions to a person you hardly knew? Discuss what you can learn about unfinished business from your past by focusing on such occurrences.

c. Be aware of transference onto the leader as an authority figure. Discuss the ways in which you might work with this therapeutically. How might such transferences block growth?

6. *Countertransference.*

a. What kind of client do you think you'd have the most difficulty working with in a group? Why? How do you imagine you'd handle a client who had very strong negative feelings toward you, especially if you felt that these feelings were inappropriate and a function of transference?

b. Select a client who you think is a difficult group member and who you anticipate will cause you problems. Become this client. Take on this person's characteristics as fully as you can. Others in the group can function as members, and one person can be the group leader and attempt to work with you. After you've had a chance to take on the role of this "problem member" for a while, explore what this experience was like for you. How did the other members respond to you? How did the group leader respond to you?

c. Identify a specific problem that you have that could interfere with your effectiveness in leading groups. For example, you may have an extreme need to be appreciated, which could determine your leadership style. Discuss this problem with your group. Although it may be unrealistic to expect a solution, you can talk about steps you could take to work on this problem.

7. *Being a group member.* What do you imagine it would be like for you to be a member of an ongoing analytic group? What issues do you think you'd want to pursue in such a group? What kind of member do you think you'd be?

8. *Role of group leader.* Review the section in the textbook on the role of the analytic group leader. What would it be like for you to work within the framework of this model? Could you function within this model if it were your primary orientation? Why or why not?

9. *Personal critique.* Devote some time to a personal evaluation of the strengths and weaknesses of the analytic approach to group therapy. What specific techniques do you think are valuable? Why? What concepts could you draw on from this model in your work with groups, regardless of your orientation? What are the major contributions of the analytic model? What are the major limitations? With what kind of population do you think this model would be most appropriate? least appropriate? Discuss how the psychoanalytic theory forms the basis on which most of the other theories have developed—either as extensions of the model or as reactions against it.

Reminder: If you've not yet read the last two chapters in the textbook (Chapters 16 and 17), I suggest that you do so at this point. The case of a group in action and the comparison of theories will help you get an overall picture of how these theories are related. As you read and study the theory chapters, the last two chapters will give you an increased appreciation of how diverse theories can be applied to the different stages of a group's development.

7

Adlerian Group Counseling

Prechapter Self-Inventory for the Adlerian Approach

Directions: Refer to page 49 for general directions. Indicate your position on these statements, using the following code:

5 = I *strongly agree* with this statement.

4 = I *agree*, in most respects, with this statement.

3 = I am *undecided* in my opinion about this statement.

2 = I *disagree*, in most respects, with this statement.

1 = I *strongly disagree* with this statement.

_____ 1. People are best understood by looking at their movement toward goals and at where they are going, rather than where they have been.

_____ 2. Group counseling is especially appropriate as an intervention, because people are strongly motivated by social connectedness and because they cannot be fully understood apart from their social context.

_____ 3. Although people are influenced by their early childhood experiences, they are not passively shaped and determined by these experiences.

_____ 4. A useful focus in group counseling is on the interpersonal and social nature of a member's problems.

_____ 5. Because people are primarily motivated by a need to belong, it is only within the group that they can actualize their potentialities.

_____ 6. Recalling one's earliest memories is an extremely important group technique.

_____ 7. People have a basic need to be superior—that is, to overcome feelings of inferiority.

_____ 8. Each person develops a unique lifestyle, which should be examined in group sessions.

_____ 9. The group counselor's goals and the members' goals need to be aligned in order for effective work to occur.

_____ 10. An analysis of each member's family constellation is essential to successful group work.

Summary of Basic Assumptions and Key Concepts of the Adlerian Approach to Groups

1. The underlying assumptions of the Adlerian approach are as follows: Humans are primarily social beings, motivated by social forces and shaped largely by social interactions. Conscious, not unconscious, processes determine their personality and behavior. People are creative, active, self-determined, and autonomous beings, not the victims of fate. They are significantly influenced by their perceptions and interpretations of past events. As they gain awareness of the continuity of their lives, they are able to modify their faulty assumptions.

2. All people have basic feelings of inferiority that motivate them to strive for superiority, mastery, power, and perfection. Their lifestyle comprises unique behaviors and habits that they develop in striving for power, meaning, and personal goals. It is influenced first by the family constellation and family atmosphere, especially by relationships among siblings. This lifestyle, which is formed early in life to compensate for specific feelings of inferiority, also shapes their views of the world.

3. The goals of Adlerian group counseling correspond to these four phases that a group goes through: establishing and maintaining the proper therapeutic relationship; exploring the dynamics operating in the individual; communicating to the individual an understanding of self; and seeing new alternatives and making new choices.

4. Adlerian group counselors make use of several assessment techniques. Assessments of the members' family constellation, relationship difficulties, early recollections, dreams, and art work provide clues to their life goal and lifestyle. The leader's task is to integrate and summarize themes from the lifestyle investigation and to interpret how mistaken notions are influencing the members. Adlerian group leaders tend to encourage members to become actively involved with other people and develop a new lifestyle through relationships.

5. Therapists challenge clients to have faith and hope, to develop the courage to face life actively, and to choose the kind of life they want. This is done largely by living _as if_ we were the way we want to be.

Exercises and Activities for the Adlerian Group

Rationale

Many of the Adlerian concepts relevant for group practice are concerned with issues such as the influence of one's family on one's current personality, reviewing one's past to determine how it has a present impact, striving for goals that define a unique lifestyle, and identifying ways of developing social interest. The basic concepts of the Adlerian approach will assume a more concrete meaning for you if you personalize them. It is up to you to decide how personal you want to be in sharing aspects of your life with others in your class or group. Remember that you can be personal without sharing your deepest and most private experiences. The following exercises and questions give you opportunities to experience some of the themes stressed in Adlerian groups.

STAGES OF DEVELOPMENT OF THE ADLERIAN GROUP

Dimension	Initial Stage	Working Stage	Final Stage
Key developmental tasks and goals	Central developmental tasks are establishing empathy and creating acceptance, setting goals and making commitments, understanding one's current lifestyle, and exploring one's premises and assumptions. The psychological investigation that occurs in the group involves exploration of the family atmosphere and subjective interpretation of childhood events.	Members are helped to understand their beliefs, feelings, motives, and goals; they develop insight into their mistaken goals and self-defeating behaviors; they work through interpersonal conflicts; and they explore the beliefs behind their feelings. A goal is to create meaning and significance in life. Through group interaction, one's basic values and life-style become evident.	This is a time when members explore multiple alternatives to problems and make a commitment to change. They translate insights into action and make new decisions. A goal is to facilitate members' awareness of their mistaken notions through observation of fellow group members and reality testing.
Role of group leader and tasks	Main goal of the group leader is to establish a collaborative relationship and to decide with clients on the goals of the group. Leader's tasks include providing encouragement, offering support and tentative hypotheses of behavior, and helping members assess and clarify their problems. Role of leader is to observe social context of behavior in group and to model attentive listening, caring, sincerity, and confrontation. Leader helps members recognize and use their strengths.	Functions of leader at the working stage include interpreting early recollections and family patterns, helping members identify basic mistakes, helping members become aware of their own unique lifestyle, challenging them to deal with life tasks, and helping them summarize and integrate what they've learned so that they can make new plans. Leader assumes that members can best be understood by looking at their strivings and goals.	At the final stage the focus is on reeducation. Leader helps members challenge attitudes and encourages them to take risks and experiment with new behavior by translating their new ideas into actual behavior outside the group. Leader's tasks include helping members recognize their mistaken beliefs and become aware of their own self-defeating beliefs and behaviors.
Role of group members	Members state their goals and establish contracts. They are expected to be active in the group and begin to assume responsibility for the ways in which they want to change. Members begin to work on trust issues, which are important in the encouragement process and in developing good morale within the group.	Members become increasingly aware of their lifestyle. They analyze impact of family constellation; they also begin to recognize that they are responsible for their own behavior. Members provide support and challenge others so that they can explore their basic inferiority feelings. Participants learn to believe in themselves.	Members are expected to establish realistic goals. They see new options and more functional alternatives. They learn problem-solving and decision-making skills. This is a time of reorientation. Members encourage one another to redirect their goals along realistic lines.

Techniques	Basic listening skills are crucial at this time. Analysis and assessment of one's lifestyle and how it affects current functioning are conducted. Other techniques include questioning, reflection, and clarification.	Some of the techniques used at this stage are confrontation, interpretation, modeling, paraphrasing, encouragement, "catching oneself" in old patterns, acting "as if," and teaching.	Basic procedures at the final stage consist of encouraging members to act and to change. Contracts are re-established, and role-playing techniques are used to help members reorient their goals. There is a continuation of the encouragement process.
Questions to consider	How can you, as a leader, establish a collaborative relationship with the members? Since Adlerians are concerned with the ways in which people strive for significance, how can the group itself be used to help members understand how they find meaning and how they meet the challenge of life? How well are the members dealing with current life tasks? Why are the members seeking this group now? What are some themes to look for in obtaining the lifestyle assessment of members? – parental influences – family information – memories of each sibling – role in the family – earliest recollections – critical turning points in life	What are the values of focusing on clients' beliefs and motives with the intention of helping them develop insight into their mistaken goals? How can early recollections and family patterns be interpreted in light of the member's current behavior in the group situation? Leaders might think of this question in helping members become aware of their lifestyle: Under what circumstances does the person acquire a particular lifestyle, and how is it being maintained currently? What are some techniques of helping members catch themselves in old patterns and begin to behave in new and more effective ways?	How can members be challenged to make a commitment to change? How can insights be translated into action? What are some ways that members can apply problem-solving and decision-making skills acquired in the group to actual behavior outside of the group? To what degree are the members behaving as active and autonomous beings as opposed to acting as victims of fate? To what extent have the members become actively involved with other people and developed a new lifestyle through relationships? Can members summarize changes in attitudes, beliefs, goals, and behaviors? Are they feeling encouraged to take risks by acting on these changes?

Reactions: Summarize your reactions to the Adlerian perspective on group developmental stages. What do you like *most*? *least*? What aspects of this approach would you incorporate in your style of group leadership?

Lifestyle Assessment

As mentioned in the textbook, Adlerians often begin a group with a structured interview to obtain information about the members' family constellation, early recollections, life goals, and childhood experiences. If you have a basic grasp of the concepts of Adlerian psychology, you can develop your own inventory for getting some of this information. Although there are set formats for the lifestyle questionnaire, the purpose of this exercise is to provide you with the experience of gathering data about yourself that you could use if you were a member of a group. I hope that by practicing on yourself, you will gain some ideas for what to look for in interviews with the members of the groups you will lead. Answer the following questions as directly, simply, and honestly as you can under the assumption that you would be interested in joining an Adlerian group *as a member*:

1. What are some of the things that you would tell others about who you are?

2. How well are you dealing with current life tasks? In addressing this question, think of the following areas: leisure, friendship, being a part of a family, relationships with the opposite sex, meaning in life, being a parent, adjustment to work, finding hobbies, your feelings about self, the spiritual dimension of your life, and any other areas you think of.

3. How have your parents influenced your life? Take each parent and answer questions such as the following:

   - Describe the parent. What kind of person was he or she?

   - What ambitions did the parent have for you?

   - What relationship did this parent have to each child in the family?

   - What were your main feelings toward the parent when you were growing up? What are your feelings toward him or her now?

   - In what ways are you similar to and different from the parent?

   - How would you describe the relationship your parents had with each other?

4. What other family information do you recall? What about your family do you think is relevant to the person who you are now?

5. Describe your brothers and sisters (from the oldest to the youngest). What do you remember about each sibling? How would you compare yourself with each sibling? Which is most like you, and in what respect? Which is most different from you, and in what way? How would you describe your position in the family? What expectations did you have for each sibling? What were their expectations for you?

6. What are your earliest recollections? What specific incidents stand out for you? Do you recall how you felt in selected situations? Can you recall any reactions that you had in these situations?

7. What do you recall about your growth and development? In addressing this question, think about specific areas such as physical development, major changes in childhood and adolescence, social development, sexual development, childhood fears, ambitions and goals, special talents, assets, liabilities, school experiences, and work experiences.

8. Can you identify any basic mistakes (mistaken, self-defeating perceptions) that you acquired in childhood or adolescence? Examples:

- Faulty generalizations, such as "Nobody really cares about me." "I am always singled out as the one nobody likes."

- Denial of your value as a person, such as "I am basically unlovable." "I will never accomplish what I want to in life."

- Misperceptions of reality: "Since people expect so much of me, I'll never measure up, and I'll always be frustrated."

9. Write a brief summary of key characteristics of your family constellation and your early recollections. From what you know of yourself, what might you select to explore in a group?

10. What do you see as your major assets? What about your liabilities? What would you most want to change in your past if you could relive your childhood?

Questions for Discussion and Suggested Activities

1. Adlerians use a technique known as "the question." It consists of asking a client "How would you be different if _____?" The end of the sentence refers to being free of a problem or a symptom. If you were troubled with migraine headaches, for example, you would be asked how you'd be different if you no longer had them. Apply this question to a specific problem you have. Explore how your life might be different without this problem. How do you think your problem may be useful to you? Are you "rewarded" for some of your symptoms?

2. What are some of your earliest memories? Are they mainly joyful or painful? Consider sharing one specific early memory in your group/class and talking about the significance it has for you. What value do you see in the Adlerian technique of having clients recall their earliest memories? Can you think of ways in which to use this technique in groups you may lead?

3. Adlerians stress birth order and the family constellation. Share with others in your class or group what it was like to be the firstborn child, the last-born, the middle child, or the only child. What does your group think are the advantages and disadvantages of each of these positions?

4. According to Adler, each of us has a unique lifestyle, or personality, which starts to develop in our early childhood to compensate for and overcome some perceived inferiority. How does this notion apply to you? In what ways might you feel inferior? Could you interpret what you do as your way to strive for mastery and significance and to overcome basic inferiority? In describing your lifestyle, consider such questions as: What makes you unique? How do you strive for power? When do you feel the most powerful? What are the goals that you most strive for? What do you most often tell others about yourself on a first meeting? How do you typically present yourself?

5. Adlerian therapists often ask group members to live "as if" they were the person they wanted to be. For example, you may want to be far more creative than you are now. Assume that you are more creative, and then describe yourself to your group. Think of other ways to present yourself "as if" you were the person whom you would ideally like to be. What stops you from being this kind of person? What can you do to begin moving in this direction? What ways can you think of to use this "as if" technique in a group? What value do you see in it?

6. Adlerians center on "basic mistakes," or faulty assumptions, that people make about themselves. These mistaken ideas lead to self-defeating behavior. For example, you may believe that to feel successful you must be perfect. Since you'll never feel perfect, you will

constantly put yourself under needless stress and experience little joy over any accomplishments. Select what you consider to be one faulty assumption that you have made about yourself or the world. Discuss in your group how this mistake affects you. If you were to change this assumption, how might your life be different? Can you identify any ways in which your basic mistakes affect the kind of group leader you are?

7. Adlerians stress self-determination by maintaining that we are not the victims of fate. Rather, we are creative, active, choice-making beings whose every action has purpose and meaning. How does this notion fit you as you look at the patterns in your life?

8. Members in Adlerian groups are best understood by looking at where they are going. Apply this statement to yourself, and talk about what direction you are striving toward and how you see your goals as influencing what you are doing now. How do you think your past has influenced your future goals? In what ways can you apply this purposive, goal-oriented approach in your work with groups?

9. An Adlerian group emphasizes developing social interest, which includes satisfying a need for social connectedness. What are some of the most important relationships in your life that meet your need for this sense of belongingness? Apply the concept of social interest to yourself by considering the five life tasks that Adlerians contend we must face and resolve: How do you relate to others (friendships)? At work, what contributions do you make, and what meaning do you derive? What sense of belonging and acceptance do you experience with members of your family and those you love? How well do you get along with yourself? How satisfying is the spiritual dimension of your life (including values and relationship to the universe or cosmos)?

10. Adlerians place a great emphasis on family processes, especially the family atmosphere and the family constellation. Consider describing what it was like for you to grow up in your family. How would you characterize your relationship with each of your siblings? Focus on what you learned about yourself and others through these early family experiences. How do you see these experiences as affecting the kind of helper you are or the kind of group leader you are?

11. What is your personal evaluation of the Adlerian approach to group therapy? What do you see as the major strengths and limitations of the model? What concepts do you like the most? the least? Which Adlerian group methods would you use?

12. What are the cross-cultural implications of using Adlerian concepts and techniques in group work? Are there any ethnic or cultural groups that you think the Adlerian approach would not be suited for? For what populations do you think Adlerian group approaches have the most relevance?

8
Psychodrama

Prechapter Self-Inventory for Psychodrama

Directions: Refer to page 49 for general directions. Indicate your position on these statements, using the following code:

5 = I *strongly agree* with this statement.

4 = I *agree*, in most respects, with this statement.

3 = I am *undecided* in my opinion about this statement.

2 = I *disagree*, in most respects, with this statement.

1 = I *strongly disagree* with this statement.

_____ 1. There is therapeutic value in releasing pent-up feelings, even if this process does not lead to changing external situations.

_____ 2. Much can be learned from acting out one's conflicts rather than merely talking about them.

_____ 3. The use of fantasy techniques in a group can increase members' awareness of themselves.

_____ 4. Group members can learn a great deal about themselves by observing and experiencing the psychodramas of other members.

_____ 5. It is important to "warm up" a group before moving into action.

_____ 6. Role playing one's own role and the role of a significant other person can increase awareness of oneself.

_____ 7. After intensive group work it is very important for members to share their feelings and discuss how they perceive the work.

STAGES OF DEVELOPMENT OF THE PSYCHODRAMA GROUP

Dimension	Initial Stage	Working Stage	Final Stage
Key developmental tasks and goals	The key task of the initial stage is the warm-up, which fosters spontaneity. This warm-up period develops a readiness to participate in the experience. Emphasis is on forming common bonds by identifying common experiences.	A major task of psychodrama is to facilitate expression of feelings in a spontaneous and dramatic way through role playing. Full expression of conflicts leads to new awareness of problems. During this phase a corrective emotional experience occurs through enactment and catharsis, leading to insight. Reality testing can follow, using a variety of techniques.	Major tasks of this phase are working through conflict situations by behavioral practice and by getting feedback, developing a sense of mastery over certain problems, receiving support from the group, and integrating what is learned into life outside the group.
Role of group leader and tasks	Director introduces the nature and purpose of psychodrama and warms up the audience (group) by using techniques. Members are briefly interviewed and asked what kind of situation they would be willing to work on. A protagonist is selected. Director's main task is to create a climate of support and prepare the group drama. Director may select a theme (such as loneliness, dealing with intimacy, and so on) that the group can focus on.	During this phase the director's task is to encourage members to enact scenes involving conflicts. Emphasis is on action, keeping the members focused on the present, and helping them fully express feelings. Director facilitates and interprets the action and encourages spontaneity and expression. Director brings members forward to take the parts of other significant figures in the protagonist's drama. Director helps these auxiliary egos learn their roles.	After the main action, director helps protagonist integrate what has occurred. Director asks for feedback and support from other members; in this way, all members get involved in the psychodrama. Care is taken so that those who participated in the psychodrama are not left hanging. Director may summarize the session and help everyone to integrate the psychodramatic occurrences. Director encourages a personal sharing.
Role of group members	Members discuss goals, get acquainted with one another, and participate in exercises to get them focused. They may decide on a theme of common interest, which in turn leads to the selection of a protagonist. Members decide what personal issues they will explore.	Members define in concrete terms a situation to be enacted; they reconstruct an anxiety-causing event from the past or one anticipated in the future. They fantasize and express themselves as fully as possible, both verbally and nonverbally. Members serve as auxiliary egos for the protagonist.	Members share with the protagonist feelings they had as the enactment took place. The sharing is done in a personal way, not an analytical way. Members give feedback to the protagonist, and they offer support. They share the personal experiences that the psychodrama reminded them of.

Techniques	The warm-up period may be directed or undirected. Warm-up techniques include the use of guided fantasy, dance, and music; the use of artistic materials; the sharing of drawings; and brief interviews of each member.	A wide range of action-oriented techniques is used. These include self-presentation, presentation of the other, role reversal, soliloquy, doubling, the mirror technique, dream work, and future projection.	After the action phase of a psychodrama, certain closure techniques may be used, such as sharing techniques, the magic shop, feedback, repeating the drama with new approaches, and discussing alternative behaviors and possible solutions to problems.
Questions to consider	As a leader of a psychodrama, how can you tap into the creativity that exists within the group? Are you alert to connecting up one person's work with others in the group as a way of promoting group cohesion? What are some ways in which trust can be established, and how can members be encouraged to participate in role-playing? How can the members best be prepared for taking an active part in the group? How can you help them to overcome their resistance to role playing? What are some ways of finding themes and concerns that most members share? Once these common problems are identified, how can you facilitate the group so that members can work on these issues together?	As the group progresses, you might ask yourself such questions as: — Do I have the courage to experiment with methods even though I do not know the possible outcome? — Do I trust my clinical hunches to try out a technique and to flow with what the member produces? — Do I have control of the group without dominating it? Are the members able to express their spontaneity and get involved? — Am I able to orchestrate all the members so that everyone plays a vital part in the group process? — Is everyone in the group involved in the process? Are some members working silently but not expressing their thoughts and feelings? How can they be encouraged to bring out their reactions?	After a psychodrama does the member have an opportunity to put into words what he or she has experienced and learned? Is care taken so that the person is not left feeling unfinished? Are some steps taken to help the member translate what was learned in the group into situations in his or her everyday life? After catharsis how can the members be helped to give words to their emotional experience? How can a cognitive component be integrated with emotional work? How can members see a link between past emotional issues and options for change of current behavior? As a leader, are you alert to ways in which others in the group might have been affected by a person's work? How can you help members attain a vision of changes desired in the future? And how can this be practiced?

Reactions: Summarize your reactions to the psychodramatic perspective on group developmental stages. What do you like *most? least?* What aspects of this approach would you incorporate in your style of leadership?

_____ 8. A group leader's task is both to encourage catharsis and to help members understand emotional experiences.

_____ 9. Group members (protagonists) should always have the right to choose what conflict they will portray, and it is their right to decide how far they will explore a situation in the group context.

_____10. Unless a group is cohesive, it is unlikely that members will risk role playing of important problems.

Summary of Basic Assumptions and Key Concepts of Psychodrama

1. Psychodrama frees people from old feelings so that they can develop new ways of responding to problems. Spontaneity, creativity, fantasy, and role playing are essential elements of psychodrama.

2. Psychodrama emphasizes enacting or reenacting events (anticipated or past) as though they were occurring in the present. It places importance on the past, present, *and* future; the past can come to life when it is brought into the here and now, as can the future. Members are encouraged to speak in the present tense and to use action words.

3. Feelings are released through verbally and physically dramatizing emotion-laden situations. After a catharsis members often gain a new perspective on an old problem, and they begin to think and feel differently about a situation. Participants gain insight and are provided with the opportunity to test reality. Group members suggest alternatives for action.

4. The psychodrama director's tasks include being a producer, catalyst/facilitator, and observer/analyzer. One of the tasks of the leader is to provide members with opportunities to challenge stereotyped ways of responding to people and to break out of behaving within a rigid pattern.

5. A basic assumption underlying psychodrama is that members of the group can benefit vicariously by identifying with a protagonist. Many people can become involved in dramatizing the individual's struggle.

6. Psychodrama has three phases: the warm-up process, which is designed to get the participants ready for the therapeutic experience; the action phase, which includes acting out and working through a past or present situation or an anticipated event; and the discussion phase, in which members are asked to share their reactions.

7. Psychodrama has many techniques designed both to intensify feelings and to bring about increased self-understanding by working through and integrating material that has surfaced in a psychodrama.

Exercises and Activities for Psychodrama

Rationale

Psychodrama is based on the rationale that therapeutic work is enhanced by dealing with problems as though they are occurring in the present. The following exercises, activities, and problems are designed to give you some experience with psychodrama; experiment with them as much as possible in your group. These exercises will help you directly experience your concerns. They can also help you increase your awareness of others' experiences and thus help you develop more sensitivity to others.

As you work through these activities in small groups, think of imaginative ways to modify them.

Exercises

1. You are setting up a psychodrama for your group. What warm-up techniques will you use? Practice these techniques in your group, and get feedback on your effectiveness from fellow group members.

2. You encourage a member of the group you are leading to role-play a situation involving a conflict with her father. She says: "I won't role-play, because that seems phony. Role playing always makes me self-conscious. Is it OK if I just talk about my problem with my father instead?" How would you respond? (You might act this out in your own class group; have one person role-play the reluctant member, and another person, the leader. Group members should take turns playing the roles, so that several ways of working with reluctance can be demonstrated.)

3. As a group leader, how would you encourage members to select significant personal issues to explore in a psychodrama without coercing them to participate?

4. Assume that a member tells you that he'd like to get involved in a particular psychodrama because he has a lot of anger stored up against women. He tells you, however, that he is afraid that if he does get involved, he will lose control and perhaps even make the women in the group the target of his rage. He is afraid he might "go crazy" if he takes the lid off his feelings. How would you respond?

5. A man in your group wants to explore his relationship with his daughter, which he describes as being strained. How would you proceed with him? What specific techniques might you suggest? What would you expect to accomplish with these procedures?

6. One of the women in the group describes her conflicts with her daughter as follows: "My daughter tells me that I simply don't understand what it's like to be 16. We fight continually, and the more I try to get her to do what I think is right, the more defiant she becomes. I simply don't know where to begin. How can I reach her?" Act out the above situation in your class or small group. Assume you are the leader, and get another person in class to role-play the mother. Consider trying these techniques:

   - role reversal (mother becomes the daughter)

   - self-presentation (mother presents her side of this conflict)

   - presentation of the other (mother presents the daughter's side)

   - soliloquy (mother verbalizes uncensored feelings/thoughts)

   What other techniques can you think of to practice in this situation?

7. Assume that the woman in the above case is role playing with another member, who is playing the daughter. All of a sudden the mother stops and say: "I'm stuck; I just don't know what to say now. Whenever she gets that hurt look in her eyes and begins to cry, I feel rotten and guilty, and I freeze up. What can I do now?" In this instance try the *double technique* (another member becomes an auxiliary ego and stands behind the mother and speaks for her). You could also use the *multiple double technique* (where two or more people represent different facets of the mother). One double might represent the guilty mother who attempts to placate her daughter, and the other double could be the firm mother who deals directly with the daughter's manipulation.

8. One of the women in your group seems aloof and judgmental. Members in the group pick up nonverbal cues such as frowning, glances and positioning of her head, and other indications of superiority. She says that people outside of the group have the same impression of her, yet she does not feel judgmental, nor does she perceive herself as others do. Assume that this woman wants to explore this issue, and use the *mirror technique*. Someone in your class group can play the role of the woman who is perceived as aloof and judgmental, and you or another member can imitate her posture, gestures, and speech. Can you think of other techniques to help this woman explore the discrepancy between her self-image and the view others have of her?

9. Think of a situation in which the use of the *magic shop technique* would be appropriate. Think of another case in which you'd be likely to employ the *future projection technique*. If possible, set up these situations in your class/group, and get practice using these techniques.

10. Select a personal problem that you are concerned about or a relationship that you'd like to understand better. (It is important that you be willing to share this problem with your class/group. If dealing with a current problem seems too threatening, consider working on a past problem that you have resolved.) Then set up a psychodrama in your group in which you are the protagonist. This exercise, if done properly, will give you a sense of what it's like to be a member of a psychodrama group. As an alternative, you can assume a role and portray a conflict. This role playing can help you identify with the problems that others might present.

Questions for Discussion and Evaluation

1. What problems, if any, would you predict for yourself as a participant in a psychodrama? What about being a leader/director of one?

2. What are the advantages of psychodrama's action-oriented methods, in which members actually act out and experience their conflicts as opposed to merely talking about them? What limitations or disadvantages do you see in this approach?

3. Psychodrama consists of verbally and nonverbally releasing pent-up feelings such as anger, hatred, despair, and so on. Do you feel able to deal with the release of your intense feelings? Have you already experienced a similar type of catharsis? Do you think that you have the knowledge and the skills to effectively deal with people who express such intense emotions? Could you deal with the emotional effects that catharsis may trigger in other group members?

4. How can cognitive work be incorporated in the emotional aspects of psychodrama? How might you help people progress by thinking about what they've experienced and putting it into a framework so that meaning can be added to experience?

5. Do you see any limitations to using psychodrama as an exclusive method in a group, without combining it with the concepts and techniques of other approaches?

6. Do you think that psychodrama has equal therapeutic value for people from all cultures? If not, for what ethnic and cultural groups do you think it is best suited? least suited?

7. What are some possible psychological risks associated with psychodrama? How would you caution group members before they participated in a psychodrama? How do you think the potential dangers can be reduced?

8. If you were using psychodrama, what steps would you take to see that members were not left with unfinished business? What would you do if a group member were left very open to intense emotions at the end of a group meeting?

9

The Existential
Approach to Groups

Prechapter Self-Inventory for the Existential Approach

Directions: Refer to page 49 for general directions. Indicate your position on these statements, using the following code:

5 = I *strongly agree* with this statement.

4 = I *agree*, in most respects, with this statement.

3 = I am *undecided* in my opinion about this statement.

2 = I *disagree*, in most respects, with this statement.

1 = I *strongly disagree* with this statement.

_____ 1. Group work best focuses on the subjective aspects of a member's experience.

_____ 2. The central issues in counseling and therapy are freedom, responsibility, and the anxiety that accompanies being both free and responsible.

_____ 3. Anxiety and guilt are not necessarily disorders to be cured, for they are a part of the human condition.

_____ 4. Being aware of death gives meaning to life and makes each person realize that he or she is ultimately alone.

_____ 5. Group therapy's basic task is to expand consciousness and thus extend freedom.

_____ 6. The meaning of death is a productive focus for group sessions.

_____ 7. The group leader's function is not to tell members what life should mean to them but to encourage them to discover this meaning for themselves.

STAGES OF DEVELOPMENT OF THE EXISTENTIAL GROUP

Dimension	Initial Stage	Working Stage	Final Stage
Key developmental tasks and goals	Focus is on how members perceive and experience their world; thus, approach is experiential and subjective. Main goal is to increase awareness of options in order to widen everyone's freedom. Initial task of a group is making a commitment to explore personally meaningful and significant issues concerning human struggles.	Members explore a wide range of universal human concerns such as loneliness, the anxiety of recognizing that one is free to make choices and that freedom is always accompanied by responsibility, the meaning of life and death, and so on. Participants consider alternative ways of dealing with issues they are facing. Emphasis is on taking responsibility *now* for the way one chooses to be. Focus is on self-discovery, which often leads to giving up defenses and living authentically.	Group counseling or therapy is seen as an "invitation to change." Members are challenged to re-create themselves. In the group they have opportunities to evaluate their life and to choose how they will change. Toward the end of a group, termination is another issue to face, for the ending of a group brings on anxiety. "Death" of a group must be dealt with fully.
Role of group leader and tasks	Leader's tasks are to confront members with the issue of dealing with freedom and responsibility and to challenge them to recognize that, regardless of the limits of choosing, there is always some element of choice in life.	Emphasis is on creating an I/Thou relationship, which entails the leader's full presence. Leader's task is to be there as a person for the members; he or she embarks on an unknown journey with the members and is open to where they will go together. Leaders must understand and adopt the members' subjective world. They also engage in self-disclosure and model authentic behavior.	At the final stage of a group, leader challenges members to go into the world and be active. Leader helps members integrate and consolidate what they've learned in the group, so that the maximum transfer can occur. Rather than "doing therapy," leader lives it through the openness of ongoing existential encounters with the members.
Role of group members	Members always have a part in the group process. They look at *who* they are; they clarify their identity and make decisions concerning how they can achieve authenticity. Members decide what they will explore in the group.	Members decide what struggles or existential concerns they will share. Typical concerns include changing roles, creating new identities when old identities are no longer meaningful, value conflicts, emptiness, dealing with loneliness, and working on the fear of freedom and responsibility.	In order to change, members must go out into the world and *act*. Since they are responsible for their own life, they decide if and how they want to live differently. If a group is successful, members achieve an authentic identity and become aware of choices that can lead to action.

Techniques	There are no prescribed techniques, and therapeutic procedures can be borrowed from many approaches. More than a group leader's technique or skill, the leader's *attitude* and *behavior* are crucial for the group's results. Group leaders are not viewed as technical experts who apply therapeutic treatment plans. There is no assessment, nor is there a predetermined treatment plan for the group to follow.	Emphasis is not so much on *doing therapy* by using techniques; rather, it is on creating an I/Thou relationship and being fully present. Thus, leaders may work with dreams; they may work with the current interaction in the group; they may explore the past with members, and they may be both supportive and challenging. Emphasis is on constructive confrontation, so that members can learn how to confront themselves.	Since group counseling or therapy is seen as a spontaneous encounter between members (and between members and the leader), the leader is free to draw on a diverse range of techniques from many other therapies. Although the focus is on the *encounter* that occurs in the group, specific techniques can be developed to challenge the members to recognize the choices they have and the decisions to make a new life.
Questions to consider	An existential group can be described as people making a commitment to begin and to continue a lifelong journey of self-exploration. Ask yourself the degree to which you are willing to embark on this journey. Are you willing to do in your own life what you ask your members to do? Are you able to experience the suffering and despair that is sometimes necessary? Are you able to tolerate the unknown, yet still take action? Can you exercise your freedom without guarantees? How do you deal with anxiety in your own life? Do you face it, or do you try to avoid it? How might this affect the way you lead a group?	To what degree are you able to be present for those in your group? Are you willing to travel down whatever paths a member might lead you? Can you adopt the members' subjective view of the world? Do you model in the group those attitudes and behaviors you hope the members will develop? What do you model? Are you able to borrow techniques from other approaches and apply them to the struggles of members? Do you use techniques within the context of the relationship that you have established with members and in the climate of trust?	Are the members willing to take action? Are they able to act on what they have learned? Are they committed to making changes in their life? How will they make certain changes? Are the members able to see that they do have choices? that there is a price to pay for acting on their choices? that they must choose for themselves in the face of uncertainty? Are they moving in the direction of trusting their decisions and relying less on others to decide for them? Are members more aware of the options for action available to them? Are they now better able to cope with the anxiety that comes with freedom than when they entered the group?

Reactions: Summarize your reactions to the existential perspective on group developmental stages. What do you like *most*? *least*? What aspects of this approach would you incorporate in your style of leadership?

_____ 8. An inauthentic existence consists of living a life as outlined and determined by others, rather than a life based on one's own inner experience.

_____ 9. The effective counselor is less concerned with "doing therapy" than with *living therapy* by being with another.

_____ 10. Therapists' major tasks are fostering self-disclosure, creating "I/Thou" relationships, and providing a model for clients.

Summary of Basic Assumptions and Key Concepts of the Existential Approach to Groups

1. People become what they choose to become; although there are factors that restrict choices, self-determination is ultimately the basis of their uniqueness as individuals. The group therapist focuses on independent choice and freedom, the potential within humans to find their own way, and the search for identity and self-actualization.

2. In the existential group basic human themes constitute the content of interactions. Existential crises are seen as a part of living and not something to be remedied. These crises frequently concern the meaning of life, anxiety and guilt, recognition of one's aloneness, the awareness of death and finality, and the fear of choosing and accepting responsibility for one's choices. Because these "crises" aren't necessarily pathological, they can't be externally alleviated; they should be *lived through* and understood in the context of a group.

3. The therapist's major tasks are to grasp the subjective world of clients and to establish authentic relationships in which they can work on understanding themselves and their choices more fully. The therapist's ultimate goal is enabling clients to be free and responsible for the direction of their own life. Therefore, the clients are largely responsible for what occurs in therapy.

4. Group leaders do not behave in rigid or prescribed ways, for they can't predict the exact direction or content of any group. Leaders are not technical experts who carry out treatment plans with specialized techniques; rather, they establish real relationships with the members of the group.

5. The *presence* of the leader, or the leader's willingness *to be there for others* and confront them when appropriate, is a major characteristic of the effective group. Group leaders must be willing to take responsibility for their own thinking, feeling, and judging. They are present as *persons* with the members, for they become active agents in the group.

6. Existential therapy is best considered as an invitation to members to recognize the ways in which they are not living fully authentic lives and to make choices that will lead them to become what they are capable of being. This approach does not focus on curing sickness or merely providing problem-solving techniques for the complexities of authentic existence.

Exercises and Activities for the Existential Approach

Rationale

The existential approach does not provide a ready-made set of techniques for group practitioners. It is more an orientation to group counseling than a system of therapeutic procedures. Practitioners can adhere to the existential perspective and at the same time use many of the other therapeutic techniques.

What follows are examples of activities that are in some way related to existential themes. Use these exercises both on your own and in your group/class, and then you'll have a better idea how to integrate existential concepts into your leadership style. Think about what you can learn about both yourself and group processes through these exercises.

Exercises

1. *Self-awareness*. Group members often say that they are afraid of learning too much about themselves. They may accept the notion that "ignorance is bliss" or that "what you don't know won't hurt you." What is your position? Are you clearly open to learning all that you can about yourself? Or do you have reservations about expanding your self-awareness? What concerns might you have about opening doors to your life that are now closed? What are some examples that illustrate your own struggles with becoming more self-aware? How do you see your willingness or unwillingness to increase your awareness as related to your potential effectiveness as a group leader? Discuss these questions in your class/group.

2. *Freedom and responsibility*. Freedom of choice entails accepting the responsibility for influencing the direction of your life. Being free means that as long as you are alive, you are making choices about *who* it is that you are becoming. Do you believe that you are what you are now largely as a result of your choices, or do you feel that you are the product of circumstances? What are some *major choices* that you've made that have been crucial to your present development? Discuss some of these crucial decisions in your group. How do you imagine your life would be different now if you had decided differently? What are some struggles that you have had between desiring freedom and fearing it? To what degree do you see yourself as being ready to accept the responsibility that accompanies your freedom? Think of specific ways in which the answers to these questions have an effect on the way you lead groups. Discuss how your concerns about your choices might affect your group leading.

3. *Anxiety*. Anxiety is not only an impetus to change but also a result of recognizing that you are responsible for your choices. What kind of anxiety have you experienced in making key life decisions? Do you agree with the existential notion that anxiety produces growth? In what situations do you experience the most anxiety? Do you tend to manage your anxiety by directly facing the consequences of your choices? By attempting to make others responsible for you? By avoiding making choices? By attempting to deny reality? In your group/class discuss how your ways of dealing with anxiety in your own life will either help or hinder you in working with clients who are also wrestling with anxiety.

4. *Death*. How well are you able to accept the fact of your own death? Do you see any relationship between how you view death and the degree to which you are living fully now? In order to clarify your thoughts and feelings about death and to examine how it affects the way you live, try some of the following exercises in your class or group:

   a. What do you think the significant people in your life would write on your tombstone? What would you like them to say?

   b. Write the eulogy you'd like delivered at your funeral. Bring it to the group and share it with other members.

   c. Assume that you knew you were going to die within 24 hours. What would you *most* like to do during these final hours? What does this say about your values?

   d. Tell others in your group what you'd most like to accomplish before you die.

   e. What are your fears, if any, about your own death and dying or about the loss of those whom you love? How do you deal with these fears?

   f. If you have lost someone close to you, consider sharing what this has been like for you. What did you learn about yourself through this experience?

g. As you reflect on your answers to the above questions, think about the implications for your ability as a group counselor to assist members in facing and dealing with the reality of their own death.

5. *Meaning in life.* Confronting our mortality makes us think about how meaningful our life is. In your group let yourself imagine a typical day in your life 5 years ago. What was it like, and what were you like then? Are there any major differences between your life then and now? Share with others in your group some of the most significant changes you've made over the past 5 years. Then project yourself 5 years into the future. What do you *hope* you'll be like then? What do you *fear* you might be like then? Explore in your group what you are experiencing in your life that contributes to or detracts from a meaningful existence. Again, how might your answers to these questions have implications for your ability to challenge clients to discover the meaning in their lives?

6. *Authenticity.* The existential perspective stresses that affirming ourselves is an ongoing process. We are authentic if we face the anxiety of choosing for ourselves and accept the consequences of our choices. Inauthentic people allow others to determine *who* and *what* they are. Discuss some crucial incidents in your own personal struggles to define yourself. Consider some of these questions as you construct your personal-identity road map:

a. Who am I? What has contributed to the way I am?

b. What roles have I typically played? How have I seen myself?

c. What choices did I make? What choices did others make for me?

d. Have I lost contact with myself by looking to others for answers and direction? Do I trust others more than myself?

e. How has my life been shaped by past actions, people, influences, and so on?

f. What more do I want from life? What kind of identity am I searching for?

g. If some of the elements that I depend on for a sense of my identity were taken away, what would I be like?

7. *Loneliness.* Share in your group some ways in which each member has experienced loneliness. Can you recall the time in your life when you felt most alone? What was this like for you? Select a poem, a picture, or an excerpt from a book that captures the loneliness you have felt at some point in your life. Bring this to the group and share it. Think of some ways to help the members of a group you are leading deal with their own loneliness.

8. *Creative solitude.* Existentialists believe that unless we can enjoy solitude creatively, we cannot develop genuine intimacy with others. Do you make time for yourself to be alone? When you are alone, what is this generally like for you? Do you welcome it or flee from it? Select a song, poem, poster, or picture that represents peaceful solitude to you. In what ways might you want to learn how to enjoy time alone? Do you have the quality of time alone that you would like?

9. *Role and functions of the group leader.* The existential approach emphasizes the role of the leader not so much as a *doer of therapy* but as a person *to be fully present* with the group members. Discuss in your group the degree to which you feel personally equipped to challenge others to look at the important issues in life. For instance, do you feel ready to challenge others to look at the choices they've made as well as the ones now open to them? Have you done this in your *own* life? Could you be psychologically present with another person who was exploring a life/death issue? Have you been willing to face such issues in your life?

10. *Personal evaluation and critique.* In your group or class explore the concepts of the existential approach that you find most valuable. What would you borrow from this approach? What are the limitations of the approach? What disadvantages do you see in limiting yourself strictly to an existential orientation? Do you think this perspective has something to offer every client? For what people do you think it is the most appropriate? What do you see as both the strengths and limitations of the existential approach in working with groups composed of culturally diverse populations? How are you able to relate in a *personal* way to the existential approach? What therapeutic techniques from other models would you apply to existential concepts in the groups you lead or will lead?

10

The Person-Centered
Approach to Groups

Prechapter and Self-Inventory
for the Person-Centered Approach

Directions: Refer to page 49 for general directions. Indicate your position on these statements, using the following code:

5 = I *strongly agree* with this statement.

4 = I *agree*, in most respects, with this statement.

3 = I am *undecided* in my opinion about this statement.

2 = I *disagree*, in most respects, with this statement.

1 = I *strongly disagree* with this statement.

_____ 1. The group members, not the leader, have the primary responsibility for the direction the group takes.

_____ 2. The attitudes of genuineness, positive regard, and accurate empathy are *both* necessary *and* sufficient for therapeutic change to occur.

_____ 3. A leader's direction is not necessary for a group to move in a constructive direction.

_____ 4. A major function of the group leader is to establish a climate of trust in the group.

_____ 5. A group leader can be effective without attending to transference.

_____ 6. Self-disclosure on the leader's part tends to increase trust and self-disclosure on the part of the members.

_____ 7. Effective group leading is best considered as a "way of being," rather than a "way of doing."

_____ 8. The group leader is more a facilitator than a director.

_____ 9. Directive intervention by the leader can interfere with the group process.

_____ 10. It is well for group leaders to avoid giving advice.

Summary of Basic Assumptions and Key Concepts of the Person-Centered Approach

1. Clients are basically trustworthy and have the potential for self-direction. The group can become aware of problems and the means to resolve them if the group facilitator encourages them to explore present feelings and thoughts. Because the group has the potential for self-direction, there is a minimum of direction on the leader's part, for this would undermine respect for the group members.

2. The person-centered approach emphasizes the personal qualities of the group leader rather than techniques of leading, because the primary function of the group facilitator is to create a climate in which healing can occur. The therapeutic relationship between group leader and members helps the members grow and change.

3. The therapeutic core conditions for growth include genuineness, or realness, of the leader; unconditional positive regard, which is an acceptance of the members; and empathic understanding of the members' subjective world. To the extent that leaders experience and demonstrate genuineness, warm regard, and accurate empathy for the members and to the extent that the members perceive these conditions, therapeutic change and growth will occur.

4. External measures such as diagnosis, testing, interpretation, advice giving, and probing for information are not useful in group work. Instead, group counseling comprises active listening, reflection and clarification, and understanding the inner world of the clients. Accurate empathy is the core of practicing in a person-centered group.

5. A basic characteristic of this approach to group work is the focus on the members as the center of the group. Members of a person-centered group are often as facilitative as, or more so than, the group leader.

Exercises and Activities for the Person-Centered Approach

Rationale

As is true for the existential approach, the person-centered approach emphasizes the group leader's attitudes far more than the techniques employed to facilitate a group. The most important consideration is the quality of the relationship that you are able to create among the members and between yourself and the members. As you practice the exercises, do your best to keep within a person-centered framework. Attempt to clarify what you hear, and *facilitate* more than *direct* the group process in these exercises.

Exercises

1. Think about what you have learned about yourself to this point that will either enhance or restrict your effectiveness as a group facilitator. What do you see as your single most important personal quality or strength? Can you identify at least one specific personal characteristic that is likely to get in the way of your effectiveness? If you are exploring these issues in a group, it would be a good idea for everyone to assume responsibility for the direction of the group. This could be an interesting exercise in itself to see what occurs in the

STAGES OF DEVELOPMENT OF THE PERSON-CENTERED GROUP

Dimension	Initial Stage	Working Stage	Final Stage
Key developmental tasks and goals	Early stage of a group is characterized by some floundering and a search for direction. Typically, members present a socially acceptable facade or reveal the "safe" sides of themselves; they describe themselves in a "there-and-then" manner. There is a milling around and a sense of confusion concerning the purpose and the function of the group. A key task is to build trust.	Negative feelings often surface over the lack of leadership. Then, a more accepting and trusting climate may prevail. Members show more of themselves, cohesion develops, and members find support in the group. Some confrontation occurs, especially when members sense that others are not being genuine. False fronts give way to a real expression of self.	The group develops a healing capacity, and members are able to move forward based on the support offered. Members develop self-acceptance; they offer feedback to one another in a climate of honesty, and a sense of community develops. Behavior changes are noticed in the group. Members show increased ease in expressing their feelings, and they gain insight into how they relate to others.
Role of group leader and tasks	Facilitator's main role is to grant freedom to members to develop a structure of their own. Leader places responsibility on members for the direction they will take and follows the direction that lead. Leader is concerned with creating a climate that is psychologically safe for the members. Leader's role is to be without a role. Central function is to help members interact honestly.	A central task of the leader is to adopt an empathic viewpoint; it is important that members feel deeply understood and cared for. Leader needs to accept negative as well as positive feelings. Leader needs to share own ongoing feelings and reactions with the group. Leader listens actively, reflects, clarifies, summarizes, links members' statements, demonstrates respect, and also shows acceptance and caring for members.	Central role of leader is to help members express how they have experienced this group and to encourage honest feedback. Leader should help members apply what they have learned in the group to life outside of it.
Role of group members	Members are expected to develop their own goals and decide for themselves how they will spend their time together. At first members are rather confused and search for a structure. They are resistant to sharing personally significant material.	Members decide what they will reveal about themselves; they express feelings to others in the group. They offer both support and challenge to others; they give and receive feedback. Members at this stage are usually willing to express immediate interpersonal feelings of both a positive and a negative nature. Self-exploration occurs on a deeper level.	Members move from playing roles to being real, from being relatively closed to being open and able to tolerate some ambiguity, from being out of contact with internal and subjective experience to being aware of the ongoing subjective process, from looking for external answers to looking inward for direction.

Techniques	Person-centered leaders tend to avoid using planned exercises and techniques to "get a group moving." They rely on the capacity of the group to decide how time will be spent. Leader's attitudes and personal characteristics are far more important than the techniques that are used.	Key techniques include active listening, reflection, clarification, self-disclosure, respect, congruence, and creation of a climate of trust. Members are encouraged to speak in an open way about whatever they are feeling at the moment. These tools do not represent techniques so much as basic attitudes/behaviors of the leader.	Leader is really not necessary at this stage if the group has been effective, for now the group is fairly self-directive and can draw on its own resources for direction. Leader may help the group members summarize what they have learned and encourage them to apply it to life outside the group.
Questions to consider	Since active listening is a basis of this approach, ask yourself how your ability to hear and to understand might be hampered. What are some barriers in yourself to hearing others? Consider the following: – talking too much and too soon – being too concerned with answers and not allowing members to explore feelings – being too quick to give advice or to look for an easy solution – asking too many closed questions – being overly directive and doing too much for the group – selectively listening or looking for ways to confirm your preconceived notions about members – paying too much attention to the content and to words and failing to hear subtle meanings	Are you able to tolerate the expression of negative feelings within a group? Can you accept in a nondefensive manner negative feelings that are directed toward you? Are you able and willing to share your own reactions in an appropriate manner with the members? Do you avoid getting caught up in roles? Are you able to be yourself in the group, or do you hide behind professional roles? Do you trust the members with your feelings? Are you able to let them know how they are affecting you? How do you demonstrate respect for the members by your behavior in the group? Does your behavior indicate understanding and acceptance?	Are you able to facilitate a group rather than direct it? Can you let the members lead the way, helping them look at their process when necessary? As a person and as a group facilitator, have you allowed yourself to be changed by a group? Are you open to growth yourself? What changes do you detect in yourself? Are you able to be both supportive and confrontive? Can you provide nurturing and challenge at the same time? Have you facilitated the group in such a manner that the members no longer look to you for direction or answers? Is the group able to function largely independently of you?

Reactions: Summarize your reactions to the person-centered perspective on group developmental stages. What do you like *most*? *least*? What aspects of this approach would you incorporate in your style of leadership?

absence of structured leadership for a session. As an alternative exercise, one or two members can assume the responsibility for being the facilitator of the group. In this facilitation do your best to keep within the framework of the person-centered approach. Allow some time before the end of the exercise to share your reactions to being a member and a facilitator during the session.

2. One of the cornerstones of the person-centered approach is accurate empathy. Use the following questions as catalysts for discussion in your class or group: What is your understanding of empathy? How can you become empathic? What are the barriers? Do you expect to have the problem of overidentification or losing your own identity by immersing yourself in another's world? What part does leader self-disclosure play in the expression of this empathy? How can you improve your ability to develop appropriate empathy for others? What kind of person do you have a hard time empathizing with, and what does this tell you about yourself?

3. This exercise is designed to help you increase your empathy for people whom you might identify as "problem group members." Think about a particular kind of person (especially a group member) whom you are likely to have the most difficulty in understanding or accepting. It can be helpful to think about the kind of group member that you hope would drop the group or, better, who would not have joined in the first place. In your class/group each member can talk about the specific behaviors of clients that present the greatest challenge to you. As an alternative exercise, instead of talking about these difficult group members assume the identity of one of these clients, and role-play that person. Each person in the group stays in the role of a problem member for most of the session. Again, two members can assume the role of co-facilitating the group by staying within the person-centered spirit. Leave enough time to discuss these questions:

   a. What was it like for you to assume a particular role of a difficult member? What did you learn about this kind of member?

   b. What did you recognize about yourself in relationship to this person?

   c. What was it like to be a part of a group that was facilitated in a person-centered way?

   d. What was the experience like as a group participant?

   e. What was it like for the facilitators?

4. Assume that you have joined a person-centered group. This is the first session, and each member has been asked to say what he or she wants from this group experience. Spend some time identifying the personal goals that would guide your participation in this group. If you were to talk about your hopes and expectations as a member, what might you say? After you have completed this exercise, spend some time as a group discussing these questions:

   a. Do you agree with Rogers' contention that the group has the capacity to move in constructive directions without structure, direction, and active intervention on the leader's part? Why or why not? What are the implications for practice if you accept this assumption?

   b. Do you agree that group members are the ones to formulate specific goals?

   c. What is it like for you to identify what you want from a group and talk about it in a session?

5. This is a group exercise that requires a collective decision about selecting a particular population for role playing. As a group, decide on a target population or a specialized type of group. Consider groups for children to increase their self-esteem, an inpatient group in a

hospital, or a support group for the elderly. Once your group has decided what kind of clients you will "become" for a session, each member needs to identify a particular role that he or she will play. For instance, if you decide to become a children's group, each person assumes a particular problem of a child for the session. As in the other exercises, two of the members can become the co-facilitators. As a conclusion to the exercise, discuss what went on within the group session. What was it like to be a part of this kind of group, and what was it like to stay within a person-centered framework?

6. After you have had a chance to try out at least one of the exercises suggested above, discuss the following questions in your class/group:

   a. *Attending and listening.* How well do you listen? What gets in your way of fully attending to others? How can you improve your attending skills?

   b. *Unconditional positive regard and acceptance.* Rogers sees unconditional positive regard and acceptance as necessary qualities for therapeutic progress. To what degree do you have these qualities? What prejudices or assumptions might you have that could make it difficult for you to accept some people? Would you put certain conditions on your acceptance of people? If so, what might some of these conditions be?

   c. *Respect.* What are some specific ways to demonstrate respect for group members? Do you think it's possible to work effectively with group clients if you don't respect them? Why or why not? What are some common ways in which group leaders can show disrespect to members?

   d. *Genuineness.* What criteria can you employ to determine your level of genuineness? Is it possible to be an effective group leader and not be genuine? What problems do you predict you might have in "being yourself" as a group leader?

7. *Role and functions of the group leader.* According to the person-centered view, the counselor in a group is more of a *facilitator* than a director, leader, teacher, or trainer. As a facilitator, you must create a psychological climate of safety and acceptance, which allows the members to use their own resources constructively. What do you think of this role? To what degree do you think you could function effectively in this role?

8. *Evaluation and research.* Rogers stresses subjective research on group processes and outcomes, consisting mainly of self-reports by the participants. What do you think of subjective measures to determine the outcomes of a group? What are some of your ideas regarding ways of finding out whether a group is successful? How would you evaluate the outcome of your groups?

9. *Critique of the person-centered approach.* Give your personal evaluation of this model, using some of these questions as a guide:

   a. What would it be like for you to facilitate this type of group?

   b. What relative importance would you assign to knowledge of theory of group process? possession of leadership skills and techniques? attitudes pertaining to the core therapeutic conditions?

   c. In what ways could you use many of the concepts of the person-centered approach in creating a therapeutic relationship and as a foundation for other approaches?

   d. What do you consider to be the major contribution and major limitation of the person-centered approach to groups?

   e. How useful would you find the person-centered orientation in working with culturally

11

Gestalt Therapy

Prechapter Self-Inventory for the Gestalt Therapy

Directions: Refer to page 49 for general directions. Indicate your position on these statements using the following code:

5 = I *strongly agree* with this statement.

4 = I *agree*, in most respects, with this statement.

3 = I am *undecided* in my opinion about this statement.

2 = I *disagree*, in most respects, with this statement.

1 = I *strongly disagree* with this statement.

_____ 1. The goal of group counseling is to help members integrate the fragmented parts of their personality enough that they can carry on the process of development alone.

_____ 2. Group work should focus on here-and-now experiencing in order to increase members' awareness.

_____ 3. Past conflicts or events are best understood by reexperiencing them in the here and now.

_____ 4. It is generally more productive to ask "what" and "how" questions than to ask "why" questions.

_____ 5. Unfinished business from the past tends to manifest itself in one's current behavior.

_____ 6. In a group setting it is important to explore the members' nonverbal messages and blocks to awareness.

_____ 7. Fantasy is a potentially powerful therapeutic tool.

STAGES OF DEVELOPMENT OF THE GESTALT GROUP

Dimension	Initial Stage	Working Stage	Final Stage
Key developmental tasks and goals	A central goal is to gain here-and-now awareness of what is being felt, sensed, and thought; group members must experiment and experience. Personal goals include achieving contact with self and others and defining one's boundaries with clarity.	Members deal with unfinished business from the past that is impeding full functioning now. The task is to integrate polarities. Group therapy is aimed at helping members give expression to the side of themselves that they tend to repress.	Members assume personal responsibility, which means that they integrate the fragmented aspects of their personalities. By achieving a moment-to-moment awareness of whatever is being experienced, members have within themselves the means to make changes.
Role of group leader and tasks	It is the leader's task to follow whatever leads are provided by group members; in this way members are able to become aware of the "what" and the "now" of their experiencing. The leader functions much like an artist inventing techniques that arise from the material in the group. Leaders use themselves as persons in the group.	The leader's task is to pay close attention to both the verbal and nonverbal messages of members and to go with what is obvious. Leader suggests experiments designed to enhance and intensify the experiences of the members. Leader pays attention to energy and helps members recognize their resistance.	After a piece of work is completed, leader may ask members to state how they are feeling. There is not much emphasis on cognitive structuring or behavior modification. It is assumed that once members gain an awareness of what they are doing to prevent themselves from fully experiencing the moment, they are capable of changing.
Role of group members	Members are expected to focus on the here and now and to reexperience past conflicts as though they were going on now. Members decide what they will explore in the group. Members are challenged to accept responsibility for whatever they are experiencing and doing. They learn to live up to their own expectations, and they make decisions.	Members are expected to directly communicate to one another and to make "I" statements. They are discouraged from asking "why" questions and instead are urged to make personal statements. The focus is on exploration of feelings. To experience these feelings fully, members take part in a variety of action-oriented activities. They don't talk about problems; rather, they act out their various roles and conflicts.	Members give and receive feedback. They have the opportunity to identify unfinished business from their past that impedes present functioning and to work through impasses. By gaining awareness of areas that were out of consciousness, they become more integrated. They are increasingly able to live with their own polarities.

Techniques	Leader uses "what" and "how" questions, but not "why" questions, to help members focus on themselves and what they might be experiencing. Leaders may use many techniques, such as fantasy approaches, asking people to pay attention to what they are experiencing physically, thinking out loud, and so on. The skilled leader avoids grabbing techniques from a bag. Rather, leader creates experiments that express what is going on in the group now.	A wide range of experiential techniques all have the general goal of helping members intensify their experiencing in the present moment. Members may explore dreams by becoming all parts of their dreams; they may engage in role playing in which they act out all the parts; or they may exaggerate a particular gesture or mannerism. Symbolic encounters are used to help members deal with unfinished situations.	Members can be asked to enact a situation the way they'd like it to be; they play all the parts. Members are often asked to give a new ending to an old and unfinished situation. Techniques help members see how past unfinished situations get in the way of effective living in the present. Members are asked to practice and experiment with new ways outside of the group. Action follows experiencing.
Questions to consider	Are you able to create a climate within the group that encourages members to try out creative experiments? Have you prepared them for Gestalt techniques? Have you earned their respect and trust? Do they see benefits in participating in a variety of experiments aimed at enhancing their awareness? Do you avoid using planned techniques to make something happen in a group? Can you follow the process and invent a technique that will highlight members' concerns? Do you take care to avoid being mechanical in using techniques? Are the methods you employ an extension of the person you are?	Do you invite members to take part in an experiment, as opposed to commanding them? Can you respect resistance in a group member? Are you able to work therapeutically with resistance? **Do you focus on what is going on within the group now? Are you able to pay attention to the subtle nonverbal messages and work with them?** Do you help members stay with their present experience and not talk about what they are thinking or feeling? Do you bring yourself in as a person, and do you respond to others in personal ways?	How can you create experiments that will help members gain awareness of what they are doing to prevent themselves from being fully in the present? How can members be helped to work through unfinished business that interferes with living now in a vital way? How can any unfinished business within the group be addressed at the final stage? **Have the members recognized ways in which they block their strengths and keep themselves from living the way they want?** Are you able to help members deal with their feelings about termination? Do you encourage them to express feelings about separation?

Reactions: Summarize your reactions to the Gestalt perspective on group developmental stages. What do you like *most*? *least*? What aspect of this approach would you incorporate in your style of leadership?

_____ 8. The most creative and effective experiments grow out of what is happening in the group.

_____ 9. The best way to deal with future concerns is to bring them into the here and now.

_____ 10. Exploration of group members' dreams is one of the leader's major methods of increasing members' awareness.

Summary of Basic Assumptions and Key Concepts of the Gestalt Approach to Groups

1. The here and now of the group members' experience is most important. The group leader focuses on "what" and "how," instead of "why," and on anything that prevents effective functioning in the present. The past, which has a significant role in shaping current behavior, is brought into the present by reenacting earlier situations that are still unfinished. Members are encouraged to reexperience unexpressed feelings of resentment, pain, guilt, and grief.

2. The Gestalt view is that people are essentially responsible for their own conflicts and that they have the capacity to deal with their life problems. Therefore, group members tend to make their own interpretations and discover the meaning of their experiences.

3. The therapist challenges group members to become aware of the ways in which they are avoiding responsibility for their own feelings and encourages them to look for internal, rather than external, support.

4. Gestalt therapists use a wide range of action-oriented techniques in assisting group members to increase their awareness. Through group interaction, it is assumed, members will become more aware of conflicts and places where they "get stuck" (arrive at an impasse), and in the group they can experiment with a variety of techniques to work through the impasse and move to a new level of integration.

5. One of the group leader's tasks is to help clients locate the ways in which they are blocking energy and expressing their resistance in their body. Through body-awareness work, members are mobilized and can take an active responsibility for their therapy. They can then be encouraged to try more adaptive behaviors.

6. Although the Gestalt leader encourages members to assume responsibility for expanding their awareness, the leader also takes an active role in creating experiments designed to help members tap their resources. The essence of creative therapy is designing experiments that grow out of the existential situation of the therapy encounter. The imaginative group invents experiments for itself that are tailor-made for what is happening in the moment. Through these experiments, members are able to confront the crises of their lives by playing out their troubled relationships in the safety of the therapeutic setting.

Exercises and Activities for Gestalt Groups

Rationale

Gestalt therapy makes use of a variety of action-oriented techniques that are designed to intensify what members are experiencing. Instead of discussing conflicts, for example, members are encouraged to "become the conflict." The idea is to fully experience every dimension of oneself (to be authentic). The Gestaltist contends that when we get close to feelings that make us uncomfortable, we tend to avoid these feelings and thus do not fully experience the various dimensions of a conflict. The Gestalt therapist will suggest experiments to help members try some new behavior and thus experience everything fully.

It is important that the following exercises *not* be done mechanically. Each exercise is best if it is tailored to the unique needs of the members in your class/group. Further, it is a good idea to give members some preparation before springing an experiment on them. Enlist the cooperation of group members by giving brief explanations of the basic purpose of each exercise. By trying many of the exercises in your own small group, you will be in a better position to know which of these techniques you might want to use when you are a group leader.

Exercises

1. *Here and now versus there and then.* Talk about a personal experience in the past tense for about 3 minutes. Then, relive the same experience as though it were happening in the present. What difference do you notice between these 3-minute exercises? What value do you see in encouraging people in groups to make past experiences into present-centered ones?

2. *Bringing the future into the now.* Are you anticipating any future confrontations? This exercise can be a form of rehearsal. Using the two-chair technique, be yourself, then become the person you expect to confront, then be yourself, and so on. Make this future event happen in the here and now. Do so briefly. When you are finished, discuss what this experience was like. What did you learn through the experiment? What are your fears and hopes regarding this future event?

3. *How do you accept and avoid personal responsibility?* Using either a go-around approach, subgroups, or dyads, have each member say how he or she avoids accepting responsibility for his or her own thoughts, actions, feelings, and moods. How can you begin to accept more of the responsibility for the ways in which you blame others for your emotional states? Examples: "You *make* me mad." "You *get me* jealous." "You *keep me* from doing what I really want to do."

4. *Identifying unfinished business.* Gestalt therapy emphasizes the role of old business that hangs around and gets in the way of our being effective and alive now. Do you have unfinished business that might limit your effectiveness in working with members' issues? What are some ways to explore your own unfinished business that could allow you to be more fully present for others?

5. *Avoidance.* The concept of avoidance is central in Gestalt therapy. How many ways can you think of in which you avoid things? Do you reach an impasse because you are afraid of feeling uncomfortable? Do you avoid changing by convincing yourself that you cannot change? Do you avoid by trying to convince yourself that you are perfectly satisfied? Do you avoid by blaming others? Try living out some of these avoidance techniques in your group. For example, really blame others for your inability to change.

6. *Nonverbal language in the group.* Exaggerate some of your typical body language. If you often frown, let yourself really get into that frown. If you have a certain mannerism, develop it fully. What can you learn from this exercise about your nonverbal language? Pay attention to others as they speak for a time, and note the tone of voice, manner of speech, quality of voice, posture, facial expressions, gestures, speed and rate of speech, and so on. What do people tell you about themselves nonverbally? Finally, each person in your group might try "becoming" one aspect of his or her body language. For example, Marilyn could "become" her tight mouth and then speak "for" her mouth: "I am my tightness. I'm holding my words back from you. I'm not going to be open, and if you want something from me, you'll have to pry me open."

7. *Experimenting with dialogues.* Each person in the group at some time might want to experiment with the dialogue technique. You can also do this at home alone. Simply put two chairs facing each other. Next, choose one of your conflicts; become one side of this conflict, and talk to the other side, which is in the other chair. Get up and sit in the other chair, becoming that other side. Carry on this dialogue for a time. If you're doing this in a group, discuss what you learned. What is it like for you to do the experiment? Which side felt dominant? Here are some examples of typical conflicts that often keep us fragmented:

- Part of me wants to open up; the other part of me wants to keep closed.

- There is the serious side of me, and then there is the fun side.

- I want to love, yet I don't dare let myself.

- Part of me wants to risk; the other part wants to play it safe.

List as many types of conflicts/fragmentations that exist inside of you as you can. Do you have trouble integrating dichotomies such as tough/tender, masculine/feminine, worthwhile/worthless?

8. *Fantasy approaches.* Try some fantasy experiments in the group. For instance, allow yourself to live out some of your expectations and fears. If you are afraid of being rejected, live out your rejection fantasies in your group. You can also use the rehearsal technique; as you think of your fantasy, repeat all your thoughts out loud.

9. *Gestalt dream work.* Try some Gestalt dream experiments in your group. For example, become all the parts of a dream. Act them out in the present tense, and let yourself really experience the dream. Or carry on a dialogue between various parts of the dream. What does your dream teach you about yourself?

10. *Making the rounds.* In this exercise a member goes around to everyone in the group and says something to each person, usually something that he or she is attempting to deny, something that is difficult to say, or something that he or she typically does not express. Make up some incomplete sentences, and experiment with making the rounds and completing these sentences. Some examples of incomplete sentences are:

- "If I were to depend on you, then _____."

- "I keep my distance from you by _____."

- "If I were to get close to you, then _____."

- "If I'm not always in control, _____."

- "One way I'd try to control you is _____."

- "If I would not smile when I'm in pain, I _____."

- "When I look at you, _____."

Any of these sentences can be selected and completed for every person in the room. It is important that you respond quickly and give your uncensored and initial reaction. After you've experienced a go-around, it would be useful to talk about what you learned from it, what it was like for you to do this, and where you could go from here. You can also experiment with making concise statements to each person in the group, using the go-around method. For example, if you find it difficult to ask for anything for yourself, you could go to each person and ask for something.

11. *Rehearsal*. Internal rehearsal saps much of our vitality. We often think carefully about the appropriate way to be, so that any spontaneity is squelched. The rehearsal technique consists of saying out loud what you are thinking silently. In this exercise select a situation in which you would typically rehash all the pros and cons to yourself before deciding what to do or say, but this time allow yourself to think out loud. In your rehearsal let yourself ham it up a bit, and really get the feel of the exercise. For example, let yourself act out in a group what you go through before you ask a person for a date. What are all the things you say to yourself? (The exercise can make you more acutely aware of how you are striving for approval or how you fear rejection.)

12. *Reversal techniques*. In this procedure you give expression to a side of yourself that rarely gets expressed. Gestalt theory holds that each person's polarities crave expression yet are often not acknowledged, much less directly expressed. For example, the very prim and proper lady in the group who continually worries about the appropriateness of her performances can be invited to experiment with deliberately inappropriate behavior. She is given permission to be *un*ladylike. The rationale here is that integration of polarities is possible if you allow yourself to plunge into the very thing that produces anxiety in you.

13. *The projection exercise*. At times people accuse others of the very things that they refuse to see in themselves. For example, you may see others as being critical and judgmental of you while failing to experience how you are very critical and judgmental of others. In this exercise you make a direct statement to others in the group and then apply it to yourself. For instance, you might say to Al "You continually expect *me* to be more than I am in here." Then turn it around and say "Al, I expect more from you in this group." Try a new statement with each person, and apply all of these sentences to yourself. What can you learn from this exercise?

14. Review all of the preceding exercises, and decide what techniques you might use in working with the following conflicts:

    - trust versus mistrust

    - the desire to get close *and* the need to pull away

    - being weak versus being strong

    - the will to risk *and* the need to play it safe

    - being appropriate versus being inappropriate

    - love *and* hate

    - the wish to express anger *and* the fear of doing so

    - dependence versus independence

    - wanting to disclose yourself *and* wanting to remain secretive

    Can you think of other conflicts or problems whose solutions might be aided by the use of the Gestalt-therapy techniques you have learned about in these exercises?

Questions for Discussion and Evaluation

1. Gestalt therapy is an action-oriented approach, one that requires the group leader to be active and employ a variety of experiments designed to enable members to intensify their feelings.

How comfortable are you in using such an approach? What is your opinion of the therapeutic value of these Gestalt experiments? How do you imagine you would respond to these techniques as a group member?

2. How do you deal with members who don't want to (or are afraid to) participate in a Gestalt experiment? If you were to invite a member to try out some new behavior and the member refused, what do you imagine you might say?

3. How would you prepare members for taking part in Gestalt experiments? What safeguards can you think of that might lessen any potential risks of Gestalt techniques?

4. What difference do you see between using preplanned techniques in a group and inventing experiments that grow out of what is happening in the group situation?

5. What uses can you see in working in a Gestalt manner with dreams in a group setting? What ways can you think of to link one member's dream work with other members?

12
Transactional Analysis

Prechapter Self-Inventory for Transactional Analysis

Directions: Refer to page 49 for general directions. Indicate your position on these statements, using the following code:

5 = I *strongly agree* with this statement.

4 = I *agree*, in most respects, with this statement.

3 = I am *undecided* in my opinion about this statement.

2 = I *disagree*, in most respects, with this statement.

1 = I *strongly* disagree with this statement.

_____ 1. Decisions about oneself, one's world, and one's relationships to others are crystallized during the first 5 years of life.

_____ 2. Once we decide on a life position, as a rule, there is a tendency for it to remain fixed unless there is some therapeutic intervention to change the underlying decisions.

_____ 3. Contracts are both basic and necessary if the group-counseling process is to be therapeutic.

_____ 4. Group members should develop independence and not rely on the group leader for guidance.

_____ 5. Relationships between the group leader and members need to be equal if the group's work is to be successful.

_____ 6. It is useful to teach group members how to explore their early decisions and parental injunctions that are influencing them now.

_____ 7. It is the leader's function to challenge members to examine the decisions they made early in life and determine whether these decisions are still appropriate.

STAGES IN THE DEVELOPMENT OF THE TA GROUP

Dimension	Initial Stage	Working Stage	Final Stage
Key developmental tasks and goals	Group therapy begins with a contract, one that is acceptable to both member and leader. Group work is guided by the contract. An early basic task is to teach members the basics of TA, including how to recognize ego states, transactions, games, injunctions, rackets, and the significance of early decisions.	At the working stage the basic developmental task is to recognize and work through impasses. Much work is done with reexperiencing early decisions and situations from childhood, with the aim of making new decisions that are more appropriate for the present. Members think about how they want to be different.	Focus at this stage is on actually making new decisions. Basic premise is that what was decided earlier can now be redecided. Members learn to thrive on positive strokes, and they recognize the power they possess. Contracts may be renegotiated, and new work may begin.
Role of group leader and tasks	Leaders begin to teach members that they are responsible for how they act, think, and feel. Leaders provide structure for the group, teach the basic concepts of TA, and may use role playing and fantasy to have members relive certain scenes. Leaders help members identify and clarify goals and develop a contract that will specify the work to be done.	At this stage the group leader assists members to recognize early decisions they made from a Child ego state. Then, from this same ego state, the members are encouraged to make new and more appropriate decisions. Leaders draw on a variety of techniques to help members work through impasses.	At the final stage of a group the leaders mainly assist members in making new decisions and life-oriented contracts; members are encouraged to accept responsibility for changing their own lives.
Role of group members	Members are expected to formulate a clear contract. They learn the ego state they are functioning in, recognize the injunctions they've accepted, and see the importance of understanding and challenging early decisions.	Members learn about the injunction/decision/racket complex. They identify life scripts. Members work through early experiences both cognitively and affectively.	During the final stage the members decide how they will change. They may use the group to practice new behaviors. Feedback and support are given.

	Techniques		
Techniques	Contracts are a basic tool. Imagery and fantasy techniques may be used. Role playing may be used to promote a here-and-now focus. The other techniques TA leaders tend to use are life-script analysis and working with injunctions and decisions.	A wide range of cognitive and affective techniques is used, including structural analysis, transactional analysis, analysis of games, cognitive restructuring, empty-chair, life-script questionnaire, desensitization. Techniques in TA groups are designed to help members feel more intensely and to think and conceptualize.	Homework assignments may be used as a way of helping the members to fulfill their contracts. Gestalt techniques may be incorporated into the TA group, as may techniques drawn from behavioral methods, psychodrama, and other action-oriented approaches.
Questions to consider	Are you able to obtain a clear and specific contract from each of the members? How can you help members formulate a therapeutic contract? Are these contracts open to renegotiation? Are the members committed to working on them? How does the structure of the group reflect the nature of the members' contracts? What would you most want to teach the members about how a TA group functions? What is your role as leader in this group? What do you expect from the members? What kind of structuring do you most want to provide? To what degree have you explored your own injunctions and early decisions? How might this influence the way you lead your group?	What kind of information would you want to include in a life-script questionnaire? How might you use this life-script checklist in your TA group? What are some techniques for focusing on injunctions and early decisions? How can you become aware of members' games, life positions, and life scripts by paying attention to their transactions with others in the sessions? How might you draw upon techniques from Gestalt therapy, psychodrama, and behavior therapy in working with concepts in the TA framework? What are some ways in which you might help members work through early experiences that have an impact on their present behavior?	To what degree have the members recognized early decisions and the life-script they have been living by, and to what extent are they making new decisions? Are they acting on these redecisions in the group? Are they taking action outside of the sessions? What new contracts might you make with members as a group approaches the final stage? How can you teach members to find support outside of the group for maintaining the changes? What are some ways to reinforce redecisions by the client and by others in the group? What are some ways to prepare members for some new situations that they will face when they leave the group? How about preparing them for dealing with setbacks?

Reactions: Summarize your reactions to the TA perspective on group developmental stages. What do you like *most*? *least*? What aspects of this approach would you incorporate in your style of leadership?

_____ 8. Game playing, by its very definition, prevents the development of genuine intimacy.

_____ 9. People tend to accept uncritically the messages they received from their parents and from parental substitutes.

_____ 10. Contracts give direction to group sessions, increase the responsibility of members to actively participate in group work, and provide a basis for equal partnership between the members and the leader.

Summary of Basic Assumptions and Key Concepts of the TA Approach to Groups

1. Based on messages that we receive in childhood, we make necessary decisions early in life that may later become inappropriate. The redecisional model of TA emphasizes that we react to stresses, receive messages about how we should be in the world, and make early decisions about ourselves and others that become manifest in our current patterns of thinking, feeling, and behaving. In TA groups the members relive the context in which they made these early decisions, and thus they are able to choose new decisions that are functional.

2. In order to make new, appropriate decisions, group members are taught to recognize ego states, to understand how injunctions and messages they incorporated as children are affecting them now, and to identify life scripts that are determining their actions. A basic assumption of TA is that we are in charge of what we do, how we think, and how we feel. People are viewed as capable of going beyond their early programming and choices by making new choices in the present that will affect their future.

3. TA is largely a didactic and cognitive form of therapy, with the goal of liberating group members from the past and assisting them to redecide how they will live based on new awareness. In a group context members can experience their life script unfolding before them through the interactions within the group. Group members represent family members from the past as well as people in the present. TA members have many opportunities to review and challenge their past decisions and experiment with new ones.

4. Members can best achieve these goals by being active in the group-therapy process. To ensure that members actively and responsibly participate, they contract to work on specific issues, and these contracts direct the course of the group.

5. TA concepts and techniques are particularly appropriate for group work. It is the leader's role and function to create a climate in which people can discover for themselves how the games they are playing support chronic bad feelings and how they are clinging to these dysfunctional feelings to support their life script and early decisions.

Exercises and Activities for the TA Approach

Rationale

Not all of the following exercises deal with therapeutic procedures routinely used by all TA practitioners; however, they are designed to increase your awareness of matters such as these: What ego state do you tend to function in? What kind of strokes do you typically receive? Which of the parental messages that you picked up early in life do you still live by? How do your decisions made early in life still influence you? What games prevent intimacy? What is the basis for new decisions?

Many of these exercises are cognitively oriented and are geared to get you to think about your assumptions and your behavior. I encourage you to think of imaginative ways of developing your own exercises; for example, experiment with combining some of these cognitively oriented TA concepts with some of the emotion-oriented techniques of Gestalt therapy. Use these exercises in your own small groups, and discuss specific aspects of this approach that you think you could use in the groups you lead.

Exercises

1. *The ego states*: *Parent, Adult, Child*. TA teaches people in groups to recognize when they are operating in their Parent, Adult, and Child ego states. Each person in your group should choose an ego state and remain in it during a group exercise. Each person should think and speak from the chosen ego state. The purpose of this exercise is to help you become aware of how you might function as a Parent without knowing it. As a variation, you might try having two group members conduct a debate between two ego states.

2. *Stroking*. TA stresses the need for strokes, both physical and psychological ones. In your group talk about the specific types of stroke that you need to sustain you. What strokes do you seek? How do you get the strokes you want? Are you able to accept positive stroking, or do you have a need to discount it and set yourself up for negative stroking? You could also experiment with asking your group members for the strokes you want. Discuss in your group the idea of conditional strokes. Were you brought up to believe that you would get strokes when you behaved in the expected manner? How does this relate to the strokes you get in your group?

3. *Injunctions*. Injunctions are messages that we have been programmed to accept—that is, messages that we have knowingly and unknowingly incorporated into our lifestyle. In this experiment each group member "becomes" his or her parent and gives injunctions. Each person should adopt the tone of voice that he or she imagines the parent would have used. Get involved in the exercise, and really tell people the way you think they should be and should live. As a second part of this exercise you might discuss a few of the following injunctions as they apply to you. What are some other messages that you heard as a child? Add these to the list. Which of these messages still influence you?

   - Don't be _____.

   - You should always do what is expected.

   - Don't feel/think/be who you are.

   - Don't succeed/fail.

   - Don't trust others.

   - Be perfect—never make a mistake.

   - Be more than you are.

   - Don't be impulsive.

   - Don't be sexy.

   - Don't be aggressive.

   - Keep your feelings to yourself.

- You ought to think of others before yourself.

- You should never have negative thoughts.

Which of these injunctions have you accepted uncritically? Which of them do you most want to modify?

4. *Decisions and redecisions.* People tend to cling to early decisions and look for evidence to support these decisions. However, TA assumes that what has been decided can be redecided. In your group devote some time to identifying your early decisions. Then, determine what you are doing to keep them current. Finally, discuss what you might do to change these archaic decisions so that you are not held back by them. For example, you may have decided early on to keep all of your negative feelings inside you, for you had been told both directly and indirectly that you were unacceptable when you expressed negative feelings. In this case you could discuss what you do now in situations where you experience negative feelings. Do you feel that you want to change your old decision?

5. *Exploring your rackets.* In TA a "racket" refers to the collection of bad feelings that people use to justify their life script and the feelings on which they base their decisions. Some possible rackets are:

- an anger racket

- a guilt racket

- a hurt racket

- a depression racket

For instance, if you develop a depression racket, you may actually seek out situations that will support your feelings of depression. You will continually do things to make yourself feel depressed, and thus you will feel this way enough of the time to be able to convince yourself that you are right to have these feelings. In your group spend time exploring how you maintain old, chronic, bad feelings. What might be one of your major rackets? List some recent situations that you put yourself in or found yourself in that led to old, familiar feelings of depression, guilt, or the like.

6. *Games we play.* In this group exercise devote some time to listing some of the games that you played as a child to get what you wanted. For example, perhaps you played the Helplessness Game. If you act helpless and pretend you cannot do something, then others may treat you as helpless and do for you what you really don't want to do for yourself. Thus, if you did not want to make your own decisions as a child for fear of the consequences, you played stupid, and your parents then did for you what you were unwilling to do for yourself. True, you did get something from the game, but how does the price you paid compare with what you got? In your group discuss some games you played as a child, then list what you got from each game and the price you paid for the gains. What games do you play now? Discuss what you get from these games. Evaluate the costs. What do you think you'd be like if you gave up these games?

7. *Life positions.* Have each person in your group briefly describe himself or herself with respect to self-esteem. Do you genuinely like and appreciate yourself? Can you feel like a winner without putting another person down? Do you think you are right and the rest of the world is wrong? Or do you continually put yourself down? Early in life you might have felt that everyone around you was just fine and that you were basically rotten to the core. What are some of the situations that led to these feelings of inadequacy? How might you challenge these feelings now? Would you classify yourself as a winner or a loser?

8. *Changes in your life circumstances.* You may have felt basically inadequate as a child, yet now you may feel very adequate in many areas of your life. What factors do you think are responsible for this shift in the way you feel about yourself?

9. *A book of you.* Write your own table of contents for a book about your life, and then give your book a title. What title best captures the sense of your life now? What would you include in the chapters? Mention the key turning points and key events of your life in your table of contents, so that others in your group will have a picture of who you are. Now, assume you want to revise your book. What revisions do you want to make, chapter by chapter? Do you want a new book title?

10. *"You are your parents" exercise.* This exercise can be done with a partner or in small groups. It will provide a format for looking at the influence your parents have on you and the quality of life you see your parents experiencing, and it will help you decide how you'd like to modify your own values and behavior. Close your eyes and see your parents at their present ages in a typical setting. Visualize the way they live. How is their marriage? How do they react to their children? What kind of life do they have? Now imagine yourself at their ages in the same setting. For a few minutes imagine that you value what they do and that your life is almost identical with theirs. In what ways would you modify the outcomes of this fantasy?

11. *Early decisions.* Assume that you are a group leader and that you determine that certain members have made the following decisions. Speculate about what factors may have contributed to each of these decisions:

    - I'll always be a failure.

    - I'm basically weak and helpless.

    - I won't feel, and that way I won't experience pain.

    - Regardless of what I accomplish, I'll never be good enough.

12. *Redecision work in groups.* Take the four statements above, and assume that each of them represents a life orientation. How would you proceed in working with each of these approaches toward life? What new decisions would you like to see made? What would it take to change these decisions?

13. *Contracts.* TA groups work on a contract basis, which means that members clearly specify what they want to change as well as what they are willing to *do* to change. What do you think of the use of contracts in groups? If you were to become involved as a client in a TA group, what are some contracts that you'd be willing to make? List one such contract, including a specific statement of some behavior you want to change and the steps you'd be willing to take to make this change.

14. *Personal critique.* What is your personal evaluation of the TA approach to group work? Consider questions such as the following in your critique:

    - To what clients do you think TA is best suited?

    - What contributions of TA do you think are most significant?

    - What are the major limitations of TA? Explain.

    - What are the strengths and weaknesses of TA as applied to multicultural populations?

    - What specific concepts from TA might you draw on in working with ethnic clients?

13

Behavioral Group Therapy

Prechapter Self-Inventory for the Behavioral Approach

Directions: Refer to page 49 for general directions. Indicate your position on these statements, using the following code:

5 = I *strongly agree* with this statement.

4 = I *agree*, in most respects, with this statement.

3 = I am *undecided* in my opinion about this statement.

2 = I *disagree*, in most respects, with this statement.

1 = I *strongly disagree* with this statement.

_____ 1. Self-reinforcement is needed if participants hope to transfer the changes made in a group to everyday life.

_____ 2. Assessment is a necessary step in the initial phase of a group.

_____ 3. Evaluation of results is best done continually during all the phases of a group.

_____ 4. For change to occur, members must actively participate in group work, and they must be willing to practice outside of group sessions.

_____ 5. Specific goals increase the chances that members will do productive group work.

_____ 6. The use of techniques cannot be separated from the personality of the group leader.

_____ 7. Groups should aim at helping participants develop specific skills and self-directed methods of changing.

_____ 8. The group leader's attention to and interest in members serve as powerful sources of reinforcement.

_____ 9. It is the group members' role to decide on their own therapeutic goals.

_____ 10. Any group techniques or therapeutic procedures are best evaluated by both the group members and the leader to determine their effectiveness in meeting goals.

Summary of Basic Assumptions and Key Concepts of Behavioral Group Therapy

1. The essential characteristics of behavior therapy in groups are as follows: the target behaviors to be changed are specified; the observable events in the environment that maintain behavior are studied; the environmental changes and the intervention techniques that can modify behavior are specified; data-based assessment is a part of the treatment procedure; and there is a focus on transferring new skills learned in the group to everyday situations.

2. A basic assumption is that all problematic behaviors, cognitions, and emotions have been learned and that they can be modified by new learning. The behaviors that clients express are considered to be the problem, rather than merely symptoms of the problem. Group therapy is seen as a teaching/learning process whereby clients are encouraged to try out more effective ways of changing their behaviors, cognitions, and emotions. The therapist does not focus on the client's past, on unconscious material, or on other internal states; rather, the focus is on manipulating environmental variables.

3. The decision to use certain techniques is based on their demonstrated effectiveness as ascertained through ongoing evaluation. All the techniques used by the leader are based on principles of learning and are geared toward behavior change. There is a wide variety of techniques, and behaviorally oriented group counselors are typically eclectic in choosing among them.

4. The group therapist is active and directive, functioning in some ways as a trainer or teacher. Some of the leader's functions include organizing the group, orienting and teaching members about group process, assessing problems and developing ways of resolving them, evaluating the progress of group sessions, planning procedures for change, modifying group attributes, and establishing transfer and maintenance programs for new behaviors. Behavioral leaders assess group problems as they arise. Data on group satisfaction, completion of assignments, participation, and attendance are typically collected and used as a basis for determining problems. Once the problems are identified and acknowledged by the members, they are dealt with by means of systematic procedures.

5. A basic assumption is that a good working relationship between the leaders and members is a necessary, but not a sufficient, condition for change. The members must actively participate in the group work and be willing to experiment with new behavior by taking a role in bringing about changes in behavior.

Exercises and Activities for the Behavioral Approach

Rationale

Behaviorally oriented group leaders use a variety of specific techniques. These research-based techniques are used systematically to accomplish particular goals, and both the group members and the leader determine whether these methods are producing positive results. If members are not

STAGES IN THE DEVELOPMENT OF THE BEHAVIORAL THERAPY GROUP

Dimension	Initial Stage	Working Stage	Final Stage
Key developmental tasks and goals	Responsibilities and expectations of both the leaders and the members are outlined in a contract. Preparation of members is stressed. At the early stages the focus is on building cohesion, getting familiar with the structure of group therapy, and identifying problems to explore. Assessment is a vital aspect, as is setting of clear goals. A treatment plan, including procedures to be used to attain the stated goals, is developed and is constantly evaluated to test its effectiveness.	Treatment plan is implemented. A wide range of treatment procedures is used to solve specific problems, and the focus is on learning skills. Central part of this phase is work done outside of the group. The group is used as a place to learn and perfect skills and to gain support and feedback so that progress continues. Much of the learning in the group takes place through modeling and observation, along with coaching. The emphasis is on behavior (changing unadaptive behavior or learning new skills) as opposed to the exploration of feelings.	At this phase the transfer of learning from the group to everyday life is critical. Situations that simulate the real world are used, so that this transfer is facilitated. Focus is on learning self-directed behavior and developing plans for maintaining and using new coping skills. It is assumed that the generalization of learning will not occur by chance, so sessions are structured in such a manner that transfer of learning will be maximized.
Role of group leader and tasks	Leader's tasks are to conduct pregroup interviews and screen members, organize the group, prepare the members by telling them how the group will work, establish group trust and cohesion, assess the nature of the problems to be explored, and provide a structure for the group. Leaders are active, and they provide information. They assist members in formulating specific goals.	Leaders develop an appropriate treatment plan based on the initial assessment, and they monitor those behaviors identified as problematic. They continually assess progress and teach the members self-evaluation skills. Leaders reinforce desired behavior, and they assist members in learning methods of self-reinforcement. Leaders model, coach, and provide corrective feedback.	Main function of leaders at this phase is to assist members in learning ways to transfer new skills to situations in daily life. They prepare members for dealing with setbacks and teach them skills needed to meet new situations effectively. Leaders arrange for follow-up interviews to assess the impact of the group and to determine the degree to which members have fulfilled their contracts.

Role of group members	Members are involved in formulating the contract. They make a list of behaviors they want to change, or they clarify the problems that they want to work on in the group. They determine baseline data for certain behaviors and begin to monitor and to observe their behavior in the group as well. The members are involved in the assessment process, which continues throughout the group.	Members report on the nature of their progress each week. Group time is used to define problem areas to work on in the group. Role playing of a behavioral nature is done to assist members in learning new skills. Members provide models for one another; they must carry out specific behavioral assignments, keep records of their progress, assess their progress in light of the baseline data collected at the initial sessions, and report to the group each week.	Members decide what specific things they've learned in the group situation, and they practice new roles and behaviors, both in the group and in daily life. Feedback is provided so that skills and new behavior can be refined, and suggestions are made for maintaining these new behavioral changes. Members act as a support system for one another. They typically agree to carry out specific assignments at the end of a group and then report back at a follow-up meeting.
Techniques	Basic techniques include contracts, checklists, role playing, and assessment devices.	Many behavioral techniques are used, including reinforcement, modeling, desensitization, cognitive methods, and homework assignments.	Feedback is a main technique, as is role playing and developing self-reinforcement systems. Follow-up sessions are scheduled to assess outcomes.
Questions to consider	Central function of leader is to create trust needed for work on issues. In doing this, leader must strive to make the group attractive to members, create many functional roles that they can play in the group, and find ways to involve all members in the group interactions. How can you best carry out these tasks? How can you help the members develop specific and concrete goals? Are the goals that are established meaningful for the members? Have they been developed by the members and the leader in a spirit of cooperation? What are specific things you expect of members?	In what ways will you assist members in assessment, monitoring, evaluation throughout the working stage? How might you involve the members in developing a treatment plan for a group? What kind of structuring would you want to provide in a behavioral group? What specific behaviors would you most want to reinforce in members? In what ways might you involve other members in one person's work? How could you use members to provide assistance to one another between sessions? What ways could you think of to use a buddy system?	How can you change your role from that of a direct therapist to a consultant during the final stage? How can you encourage the members to assume an increasing share of the leadership tasks? What self-help skills and problem-solving strategies would you want to teach members as a group is approaching termination? What kinds of short-term and long-term follow-up sessions might you consider setting up before a group ends? Along with members, how can you evaluate the effectiveness of a given group?

Reactions: Summarize your reactions to the behavioral perspective on group developmental stages. What do you like *most? least?* What aspects of this approach would you incorporate in your leadership style?

making progress, the therapeutic procedures can be modified. It is basic to the behavioral approach that therapeutic procedures and evaluation of these techniques proceed simultaneously.

Most of the behavioral techniques are designed to effect specific behavioral changes—that is, either to decrease or eliminate undesirable behaviors or to acquire or increase desired behaviors. The following exercises will show you ways in which to use learning principles in your work to change behavior. You can apply many of the techniques presented in these exercises to your own life. As you experiment with these techniques in your small group or in class, determine which aspects of the behavioral approach you would incorporate in your work as a group leader, regardless of the theoretical model you might be working with.

Exercises

1. *Setting up a behavioral group.* Assume that you are a behaviorally oriented group leader and are giving a talk to a community gathering where you hope to begin a group. What points would you emphasize to give these people a good picture of your group, your functions and role as a leader, and the things that would be expected of them as participants? Assume that they respond enthusiastically and want to join your group. Where would you begin, and how would you proceed in setting up this group? What pregroup concerns would you have? What would you do during the initial meeting?

2. *Terminating and evaluating a group.* Assume that the above group meets for 20 weeks. It is now the 18th week. What would you be concerned with as a group leader? Mention specific issues that you'd want the group to deal with. What evaluation procedures would you employ at the end of the group? What follow-up procedures would you use?

3. *Group leaders as skilled technicians.* Behavioral group leaders must be skilled technicians who also possess the human qualities that lead to the climate of trust and care necessary for the effective use of therapeutic techniques. From a behavioral perspective what emphasis would you place on your relationships with the members of your groups? What specific skills do you see yourself as having that would be useful in a behavioral group? What are a few examples of skills that you would either like to acquire or refine as ways of enhancing your ability to function from a behavioral perspective?

4. *Relaxation exercises.* Many behavioral group therapists use self-relaxation techniques. Members are taught how to systematically relax every part of their body. They practice in the group and also at home on a daily basis. In your own group one member can volunteer to lead a tension/relaxation procedure, going from head to foot. After the exercise discuss the possibilities for using relaxation procedures in any group. What are the values of such procedures? Consider practicing these exercises to reduce stress. Give them at least a 3-week trial to determine some personal benefits.

5. *Social reinforcement.* Observe in your own class or group how social reinforcement works. For what are members reinforced? Pay attention to *nonverbal* responses, such as smiles, head nodding, and body posture, as well as verbal support and approval. Do you see ways in which you can systematically use social reinforcement in a group situation? What social reinforcers have the most impact on your behavior? Support? Compliments? Applause?

6. *Modeling.* Consider the importance that you place on your role as a leader in modeling for members. Consider factors such as clear and direct speech, self-disclosure, respect, enthusiasm, sensitivity, and caring confrontation. In your group discuss ways in which you can model positive behavior. Also, observe the effect of a certain behavior on your group (for example, speaking enthusiastically). Do you notice that members tend to assume some of the traits of the leader? What are the implications of this influence? In addition to your own modeling as a group leader, the participants can function as models. Since people tend to imitate more rapidly and thoroughly those with whom they share common features,

modeling by peers in the group enhances observational learning on the part of other members. In what ways can you shape a group norm for this type of modeling? What are some behaviors that you would like to see modeled in your groups?

7. *Social-skill training in groups: an introduction.* Assume that you are giving a talk to people who might be interested in joining the social-skill-training group that you are forming. What would you tell them about your group? What are some examples of social skills that members might learn and practice? Whom is the group for? How can it help them? What would they do in this group? What are some of the techniques that you'd use during the group sessions? For this exercise, two of those in your group can be the co-leaders and explain the group to the potential members; the others in the group can ask questions relating to what they will be expected to do in the group, how these activities will help them in daily life, and how they can apply what they learn.

8. *Applying assertiveness-training procedures to yourself.* In an exercise related to the preceding one, think of an area where you have difficulty being assertive. This difficulty may involve dealing with supervisors, returning faulty merchandise, or expressing positive feelings. In your own group you can experiment with improving your assertiveness in this area, using specific procedures that are described in the textbook such as behavior rehearsal, role playing, coaching, cognitive restructuring, and so on. Practice with these procedures *as a member* first, so that you can get some idea of the values and applications of assertive-behavior training.

9. *Stress-management training in groups.* Review the section in the textbook on a group approach to stress management, especially Meichenbaum's stress-inoculation-training program. Think about yourself as a participant in such a training group. What are a couple of factors in your life that contribute to your experience of stress? Identify some of your cognitions (beliefs or self-talk) that play a role in creating and maintaining stress. Consider keeping an open-ended diary in which you systematically record specific thoughts, feelings, and behaviors for at least 2 weeks. This process can be useful in teaching you to become aware of your own role in creating your stress. If you are in a group at this time, consider bringing into a session a specific concern about stress. After working on this concern in your group, develop a plan that will lead to practice in daily situations. Assume that you want to begin a stress-management group in the agency you work for. What specific steps would you take in forming this group? What behavioral techniques would you use? How would you explain the purpose of your group to prospective members?

10. *Working on specific goals.* A real value of the behavioral approach is its specificity—its ability to translate broad goals into specific ones. State some broad goals that you'd like to attain. Then, in your group, practice making these goals concrete. Make them specific to the degree that you actually *know* what it is that you want and can thus measure progress toward them. As a second part of this exercise, assume that members in one of your groups make broad and vague statements such as the following. Can you think of ways to make these goals clear and concrete?

a. "I'd like to be more spontaneous." Concrete goal is: _____

_____

_____

b. "I need to learn how to get in touch with my feelings." Concrete goal is: _____

_____

_____

c. "My goal is to become a more autonomous and actualized person." Concrete goal is: _____

_____

_____

d. "I have many fears that get in my way of living the way I want." Concrete goal is: _____

_____

_____

e. "I'd like to be able to relate better." Concrete goal is: _____

_____

_____

f. "I'm all messed up, and I need a major overhaul." Concrete goal is: _____

_____

_____

g. "My goal is to get to know myself better." Concrete goal is: _____

_____

_____

11. *Groups designed for self-directed change.* Assume that you want to organize a group for people who are interested in self-directed change. For example, they may be interested in stopping smoking, taking weight off and keeping it off, or improving their self-discipline in study or work. How would you design a group of this nature?

12. *Applying a self-directed program to yourself.* In your group or class discuss the specific behavior that you want to work on during the semester. Next, decide what you are willing to do to change this behavior. Draw up a specific contract, and include details. (For instance, "I will lose 10 pounds by the end of the semester, regulate my eating habits, and ride a bicycle for an hour a day for the rest of the semester.") Then, practice your program, and report your progress to your group. Ask a fellow student to support you if you get discouraged or find that you have difficulty sticking to your program. You can apply self-directed behavior-modification methods to areas such as developing better patterns of organization, reducing stress through meditation and relaxation exercises, changing what you consider to be negative behavior patterns, and so on.

13. *Cognitive restructuring in groups.* Identify a few major cognitions that have a negative impact on the way people behave. Think of common self-defeating statements that you have heard. Can you think of some methods for helping group members challenge negative cognitions and also develop a new and more effective set of beliefs and thoughts? Can you think of possible homework assignments to supplement the work done in the group sessions? What steps might you suggest to members in learning new ways of thinking?

14. *Self-reinforcement methods.* Behavioral group work teaches members how to reinforce themselves so that they are not dependent on external rewards to maintain newly acquired skills. In your class/group experiment with ways in which you can *reinforce yourself* after successes. Brainstorm this topic in your group. Self-reinforcement may involve learning

ways to praise yourself *and* at the same time remind yourself of certain realities that you tend to forget. An example of this is writing notes to yourself and putting them on the mirror. These notes could say "I am worthwhile," "I *am* enough," "I have a right to my own feelings," "I'll like myself better if I treat myself with regard," "I can take time for myself."

15. *Personal evaluation and critique of behavioral groups.* Discuss in your class/group what you consider to be the major strengths and weaknesses of the behavioral approach to groups. Consider such questions as these:

a. What learning principles apply to all groups?

b. How can any group leader (regardless of theoretical orientation) draw on behavioral concepts and procedures?

c. How would you feel about using behavioral techniques as a group leader?

d. If you were leading a group composed of members with culturally diverse backgrounds, what behavioral techniques do you think might be particularly effective?

e. What do you see as the major strengths and limitations of behavioral group approaches in working with multicultural populations?

f. From a behavioral perspective what kind of teaching would you want to do if you were beginning a group with culturally diverse clients?

g. What concepts and techniques do you think are most useful from this approach?

h. What are the limitations of behavior therapy?

i. What are your criticisms?

Ethical Principles and Guidelines for Assertiveness Training

As assertion training has gained popularity in the last few years, responsible practitioners have expressed concern about the possible misuse of this counseling technique. Some of the areas of concern are unqualified trainers, illegitimate purposes, and application in inappropriate circumstances. A statement of "principles for ethical practice of assertive-behavior training," developed by a group of nationally recognized assertiveness-training professionals, is presented in *Your Perfect Right: A Manual for Assertiveness Trainers* (by R. E. Alberti & M. L. Emmons, 1986). This document has important implications for those who lead assertiveness-training groups, especially with regard to the issue of client self-determination. Here are some of the specific guidelines contained in the above statement. Clients should be

- fully informed in advance of all procedures to be utilized

- given the freedom to participate or not to participate in certain activities

- provided with clear definitions of assertive behavior and assertiveness training

- fully informed of the education, training, experience, and qualifications of the leader(s)

- told what the goals and potential outcomes of assertiveness training are, including the risks involved and possible negative reactions from others

- made clearly aware of the respective responsibilities of leader(s) and client(s)

- informed of the ethical guidelines concerning confidentiality in the specific training setting

Alberti and Emmons make the point that appropriate consideration should be given to the limitations and contraindications of this approach. Some of the client considerations they suggest are these:

- Make a careful assessment to determine whether a given client should be in individual or group work.

- Clients who are highly anxious should be treated for anxiety before being placed in a training group.

- Unmotivated clients not only are unlikely to make progress themselves but also may discourage other members.

- Actively resistant clients are likely to sap the energy of a group.

- Extremely aggressive individuals should be screened out.

A central ethical issue pertains to the level of training of the person leading an assertiveness-training or a social-skill-training group. Alberti and Emmons summarize the qualifications for trainers. These groups can be conducted as education, as skill building, or as therapy, and the depth of the leader's interventions should be limited to those procedures that he or she is qualified to administer.

If you would like more-detailed information about ethical and practical issues in designing and conducting these groups, *The Professional Edition of Your Perfect Right: A Manual for Assertiveness Trainers* (Alberti & Emmons, 1986) is highly recommended.

14

Rational-Emotive Group Therapy

Prechapter Self-Inventory for Rational-Emotive Therapy

Directions: Refer to page 49 for general directions. Indicate your position on these statements, using the following code:

5 = I *strongly agree* with this statement.

4 = I *agree*, in most respects, with this statement.

3 = I am *undecided* in my opinion about this statement.

2 = I *disagree*, in most respects, with this statement.

1 = I *strongly disagree* with this statement.

_____ 1. Our beliefs are the primary cause of emotional disturbances; therefore, an appropriate focus of group work is on examining these beliefs.

_____ 2. For group leaders to be effective, they need to challenge and convince members to practice activities both inside and outside the group.

_____ 3. It is the group leader's task to show members *how* they have caused and are perpetuating their emotional/behavioral problems.

_____ 4. Because we have a tendency to easily make and keep ourselves emotionally disturbed, we are likely to sabotage our best efforts at changing.

_____ 5. Once irrational beliefs are discovered, they can be counteracted in a variety of ways and replaced.

_____ 6. A large part of the leader's task is to be a teacher, especially of ways to detect and dispute irrational beliefs.

STAGES IN THE DEVELOPMENT OF THE RATIONAL-EMOTIVE THERAPY GROUP

Dimension	Initial Stage	Working Stage	Final Stage
Key developmental tasks and goals	Key task is to teach members the A-B-C theory of how they create and can "uncreate" their own disturbances, how they can detect their irrational beliefs, and how they can attack these faulty beliefs. Members need to learn that situations themselves do not cause emotional problems; rather, their beliefs about these situations cause the problems. Thus, changing beliefs (not situations) is the road to improvement.	Group focuses on the identification and attacking of members' "musts," "shoulds," and "oughts." Members learn that if life is not the way they want it to be, this may be unfortunate but not catastrophic. In place of self-defeating assumptions, members incorporate beliefs that are grounded in reality. Members learn a variety of ways to continue challenging their *musturbatory* philosophy.	Ultimate aim is that participants internalize a rational philosophy of life, just as they internalized a set of irrational beliefs. This phase is one of reinforcement of new learning to replace old patterns. Emphasis is on teaching people better methods of self-management. It is important for members to commit themselves to continue to work and practice new behavior in real life.
Role of group leader and tasks	Group leader shows members *how* they have caused their own misery by teaching them the connection between their emotional-behavioral disturbances and their beliefs. Leader teaches members how to dispute irrational beliefs.	Leader acts as a counterpropagandist who confronts members with the propaganda they originally accepted without question and with which they continue to indoctrinate themselves. Leader strives to modify members' thinking by challenging their underlying basic assumptions about reality.	Therapist continues to act as teacher by showing members methods of self-control, giving them homework assignments that involve active practice in real life, and correcting any lasting faulty patterns.
Role of group members	Members need to be willing to discipline themselves and work hard, both during the sessions and between sessions. They must be active, both in and out of the group, for they learn by practicing and doing.	Members learn how to analyze, dispute, and debate by using scientific methods to question their belief systems. Members ask "What evidence supports my views?" Members learn a new, rational set of beliefs.	Group members integrate what they have learned and continue to make plans for how they can practice overcoming self-defeating thinking and emoting outside of the group.

	Techniques		
Techniques	Educational methods: use of tapes, books, and lectures; suggestions; information giving; interpretation; group feedback and support; other directive, confrontational, didactic, philosophic, and action-oriented methods. Therapist employs a wide range of cognitive, emotive, and behavioral techniques to fit the needs of the client.	A rapid-fire and forceful set of techniques, which emphasize cognitive factors, is used. These include use of persuasion, homework assignments, desensitization, role playing, modeling and imitation, behavior rehearsal, operant control of thinking and emoting, group feedback and support, cognitive restructuring, and assertive training.	Continued use of emotive-evocative and cognitive behavioral techniques that people can use on their own after therapy terminates. Members can continue working with and practicing new ways of thinking and behaving as they encounter new problems.
Questions to consider	What would you want to teach members about the ways they create their own disturbances? What are some common irrational beliefs that you might expect members to bring to a group? In what ways do you think a member's belief system is connected to how the person behaves and feels? How can you confront members to recognize their irrational thinking without adding to their defensiveness? What kind of relationship would you want to create with the members before you attempted to use forceful and directive procedures? What behavioral techniques would you employ in a RET group at the early stage?	To what degree have you recognized and challenged your own "musts," "shoulds," and "oughts"? To what extent have you looked at your self-defeating assumptions and behavior? Do you agree that the role of leader is to act as a counterpropagandist who confronts members with beliefs they have accepted without thinking and questioning? What are some specific methods you might teach the members in learning how to analyze, dispute, and debate unexamined assumptions? What are some examples of RET homework that you are likely to use during the working stage? Can you keep from imposing your values on members? Do you challenge them to think for themselves?	If you employ directive strategies and encourage members to take a specific course of action, are you clear about your own motives? Are you willing to state your motivations to your clients? Do you share with them your values that pertain to choices they might make? How can you teach members ways to maintain constructive thinking once they leave a group? How can you help members maintain gains they have made in challenging self-defeating attitudes? Might you want to integrate any other therapeutic techniques from other approaches during the final stages? If so, what? What are some ways that you could evaluate the effectiveness of your group as it moves toward termination?

Reactions: Summarize your reactions to the rational-emotive approach to group developmental stages. What do you like *most?* *least?* What aspects of this approach would you incorporate in your leadership style?

_____ 7. Homework assignments are a valuable part of group counseling.

_____ 8. Effective therapy includes cognitive, emotional, and behavioral elements.

_____ 9. A major function of the group leader is to enable members to recognize their "shoulds," "oughts," and "musts."

_____ 10. A warm and personal relationship between the group leader and the members is not essential to the group's success.

Summary of Basic Assumptions and Key Concepts of the Rational-Emotive Approach to Groups

1. People's belief systems cause emotional disturbances. Situations alone do not determine emotional disturbances; rather, it is people's evaluations of these situations that are crucial. People have a tendency to fall victim to irrational beliefs, and although these beliefs were originally incorporated from external sources, people internalize and maintain them by self-indoctrination.

2. The leader plays the role of a teacher and not that of an intensely relating partner. RET stresses the importance of the therapist giving and showing unconditional acceptance of members, even when they act badly in and out of the group. It emphasizes the group therapist's skill in challenging, confronting, and convincing the members to practice activities that will lead to positive change. RET employs a wide variety of cognitive, behavioral, and emotive techniques, and it is therefore a truly eclectic approach to group therapy.

3. In order to overcome the indoctrination process that results in irrational thinking, group therapists use active cognitive methods such as disputing, teaching, persuading, and reindoctrinating to get group members to substitute a rational belief system.

4. Emotive methods in RET groups are aimed at alleviating emotional disturbances. It is assumed that the best way to change feelings is by changing self-defeating thoughts. Some emotive techniques include role playing, unconditional acceptance, rational-emotive imagery, and shame-attacking exercises.

5. Behavioral methods in RET groups are designed to motivate members to take actions that will result in thinking and feeling differently. RET stresses that meaningful cognitive change is unlikely unless clients are willing to behave differently. Some of the techniques include behavioral homework assignments, use of reinforcements and penalties, skills training, and feedback.

Exercises and Activities for the RET Approach to Groups

Rationale

The rationale underlying most of these exercises and RET techniques is that most of us make irrational assumptions about ourselves and the world that lead to emotional/behavioral disturbances. The essence of RET is that rational thinking can lead to more effective living. To combat stubborn and persistent irrational beliefs, it is necessary to work and practice diligently and to replace faulty thinking with logical thinking.

The following activities and exercises are designed to help you experience the process of challenging your own thinking and to become aware of the consequent feelings of your belief system.

As you work through these exercises on your own, with another person, and with a small group, think about ways in which you, as a group leader, could incorporate them into group practice.

Exercises

1. Make a list of a few self-defeating sentences that you tend to say to yourself. The purpose of this exercise is for you to become aware of how *you* continue to indoctrinate yourself with propaganda. Then take your self-defeating sentences and rewrite them in new and constructive ways, much like the example that follows:

   a. *Self-defeating sentence*: "I'm sure I'll be a failure as a counselor."

   b. *Constructive sentence*: "If I'm willing to work diligently and apply myself to a good training program, I'm sure that with experience I'll succeed."

   a. Self-defeating sentence: _____

   _____.

   b. Constructive sentence: _____

   _____.

   a. Self-defeating sentence: _____

   _____.

   b. Constructive sentence: _____

   _____.

2. Write similar constructive sentences that you might suggest to a group member who repeated self-defeating sentences such as the following:

   a. "I've always been stupid, and I suppose I'll always be that way."

   b. _____.

   a. "I need to please everyone, because rejection is just terrible."

   b. _____.

   a. "Because my parents never really loved me, I guess nobody else could ever love me."

   b. _____.

   a. "Basically, I'm simply an irresponsible person."

   b. _____.

3. *Self-rating*—giving yourself a "good" or "bad" evaluation based on your performances—can influence the way you think and feel. Ellis contends that the self-rating process constitutes one of the main sources of people's emotional disturbances. Discuss these questions in class or in a small group.

   a. What are some of the ways you rate yourself?

b. How do you *feel* when you rate yourself critically?

4. *Homework assignments* are an integral part of RET group work. Think of your own patterns of behavior and ways that you'd like to think, feel, and behave more rationally. Then list a few specific homework assignments that you could do to challenge yourself to accomplish this. Carry out a few of these assignments, and bring the results to your group. Ask for suggestions from your fellow students/group members. Below are a couple of examples of homework assignments that may be useful to you.

   a. Do you have difficulties in making social contacts? Does it make you anxious to initiate a discussion with a member of the opposite sex? Do you want to feel more at ease in these situations than you do now? If so, try this experiment: Go to each of your classes early and sit in a different place each time near a person whom you don't know. Push yourself to initiate a conversation. Keep a record of all of the things, including irrational beliefs, you rehearse in your head before you make these contacts.

   b. Are you troubled by conflicts with authority figures? For example, would you like to feel easier about approaching an instructor to discuss your progress in the course? If so, what stops you from selecting at least one instructor and making the time and effort to discuss with him or her matters that are of importance to you?

5. Think of some in-group assignments or homework exercises for members who demonstrate problems such as the following, and write them down. Bring these assignments to your class or group, and share ideas with one another.

   a. A woman says very little during the group sessions, because she's afraid that she'll sound stupid and that other members will laugh at her. One possible assignment is:

   _____

   _____

   _____

   b. A woman believes that men are always judging her in a critical fashion. She avoids me, both in the group and outside of it, because she doesn't want to feel negatively judged. One possible assignment is:

   _____

   _____

   _____

   c. One of the members of a group you're leading tells you that he feels and believes that he *must* gain universal approval. When someone is displeased with him, he feels like a worm. Because of this he tries hard to figure out what every person in the group wants from him, and then he goes out of his way to meet these expectations. He says he is sick of being the "super nice guy" and desperately wants to change. One possible assignment is:

   _____

   _____

   _____

112

d. A member describes her drive to be perfect and says that she carefully avoids situations and activities that make it difficult for her to feel that she's performed perfectly. She wants to relax and not be obsessed with the thought that she *must* be perfect in anything she attempts. One possible assignment is:

_____

_____

_____

6. Role playing with a cognitive focus can be useful in an RET group. Think of a situation that causes you difficulty—one that you'd be willing to share in your group or class—and role-play it. For example, you may feel victimized because you can't get your father's approval. Have a person play *your* role first, and you role-play your demanding father who refuses to give approval no matter what is accomplished. After about 5 minutes or so, reverse roles: you be yourself while someone else plays your father as you portrayed him. Continue this for about another 5 minutes. Afterward, do a *cognitive evaluation* of this interchange in your group. Some questions you might include in your evaluation are:

a. How did you appear to others as you played yourself talking with your father?

b. Do you *need* his approval to survive?

c. What will become of you if he never gives you his approval?

d. What might you have to do to get his approval?

e. How do you imagine you'd feel if you did what might be required to gain his acceptance?

f. Can you gain self-acceptance, even if acceptance is not forthcoming from him?

g. In what ways do you treat others like your father?

7. Imagine that you want to conduct an RET group in the agency or institution in which you work (or may someday work in the future). Convince your supervisor or the agency director of the advantages of doing RET in a *group* over doing it on an individual basis. What are some unique advantages of RET in groups, and why should your supervisor permit you to organize such a group? This can be a productive exercise in your group or class. Another student can play the role of the director/supervisor of the agency.

8. This exercise is designed to help you identify and explore some possible irrational beliefs that you hold as a helper or a group leader. Review the list below, and circle those items that most apply to you.

a. I expect myself to be successful with all of my clients all of the time.

b. I must be an outstanding group leader.

c. It would be terrible if I made a mistake in the groups I lead.

d. I feel I need the approval of virtually all the people in my group.

e. If a group session does not go well, I typically feel responsible and guilty.

f. If a group member stops coming to the sessions, I tend to blame myself.

g. I must always be available for all my clients who might need me.

h. If a participant in my group is in pain, I should take it away.

i. I should know everything.

j. If I make a mistake, that means I'm a failure.

k. I frequently expect myself to be perfectly competent in leading groups.

After you've identified a few of the above statements that you most often say, practice methods of disputing them. Also, attempt to replace the irrational belief with a rational and effective belief. For example, if you say "I must be approved or accepted by all of the members of my group," a disputation might include: "Where is it written that my own approval depends on getting approval from others? If a client disapproves of me, can't I still feel like a worthwhile person and group leader?" An example of a rational and effective belief is "While it's true that I don't enjoy disapproval, I can tolerate it. I don't have to be accepted by everyone in order to feel accepted by myself." Spend some time in your group discussing how some of your beliefs actually interfere with your effectiveness as a group leader.

9. In your class/group discuss what you consider to be some of the major advantages and disadvantages of employing RET techniques in working with culturally diverse groups. Specifically, what cultural variables would you want to take into account in applying them?

10. *RET Self-Help Form.* The form is reproduced here by permission of the Institute for Rational-Emotive Therapy. For at least a week, pay attention to any situations that are problematic for you. Use the form to record at least one event that contributes to an emotional upset or some self-defeating behavior. Then use the form to identify any irrational beliefs that you hold about a particular event; dispute each irrational belief, and replace it with a rational belief. Bring the completed form to your class/group the following week, and use it as a basis for talking about how your beliefs influence the way you feel and what you do.

RET SELF-HELP FORM

Institute for Rational-Emotive Therapy
45 East 65th Street, New York, N.Y. 10021
(212) 535-0822

(A) ACTIVATING EVENTS, thoughts, or feelings that happened just before I felt emotionally disturbed or acted self-defeatingly: _____

_____

(C) CONSEQUENCE or CONDITION—disturbed feeling or self-defeating behavior—that I produced and would like to change: _____

_____

(B) BELIEFS—Irrational BELIEFS (IBs) leading to my CONSEQUENCE (emotional disturbance or self-defeating behavior). Circle all that apply to these ACTIVATING EVENTS (A).	(D) DISPUTES for each circled IRRATIONAL BELIEF. Examples: "Why MUST I do very well?" "Where is it written that I am a BAD PERSON?" "Where is the evidence that I MUST be approved or accepted?"	(E) EFFECTIVE RATIONAL BELIEFS (RBs) to replace my IRRATIONAL BELIEFS (IBs). Examples: "I'd PREFER to do very well but I don't HAVE TO." "I am a PERSON WHO acted badly, not a BAD PERSON." "There is no evidence that I HAVE TO be approved, though I would LIKE to be."
1. I MUST do well or very well!		
2. I am a BAD OR WORTHLESS PERSON when I act weakly or stupidly.		
3. I MUST be approved or accepted by people I find important!		
4. I NEED to be loved by someone who matters to me a lot!		
5. I am a BAD, UNLOVABLE PERSON if I get rejected.		
6. People MUST treat me fairly and give me what I NEED!		

(OVER)

7. People MUST live up to my expectations or it is TERRIBLE!		
8. People who act immorally are undeserving, ROTTEN PEOPLE!		
9. I CAN'T STAND really bad things or very difficult people!		
10. My life MUST have few major hassles or troubles.		
11. It's AWFUL or HORRIBLE when major things don't go my way!		
12. I CAN'T STAND IT when life is really unfair!		
13. I NEED a good deal of immediate gratification and HAVE to feel miserable when I don't get it!		
Additional Irrational Beliefs:		

(F) FEELINGS and BEHAVIORS I experienced after arriving at my EFFECTIVE RATIONAL BELIEFS: _____

I WILL WORK HARD TO REPEAT MY EFFECTIVE RATIONAL BELIEFS FORCEFULLY TO MYSELF ON MANY OCCASIONS SO THAT I CAN MAKE MYSELF LESS DISTURBED NOW AND ACT LESS SELF-DEFEATINGLY IN THE FUTURE.

Joyce Sichel, Ph.D. and Albert Ellis, Ph.D.
Copyright © 1984 by the Institute for Rational-Emotive Therapy. Reprinted by permission.

100 forms $10.00
1000 forms $80.00

15

Reality Therapy in Groups

Prechapter Self-Inventory for Reality Therapy

Directions: Refer to page 49 for general directions. Indicate your position on these statements, using the following code:

5 = I *strongly agree* with this statement.

4 = I *agree*, in most respects, with this statement.

3 = I am *undecided* in my opinion about this statement.

2 = I *disagree*, in most respects, with this statement.

1 = I *strongly disagree* with this statement.

_____ 1. The group counselor's main task is to encourage the members to face reality and make value judgments about their behavior.

_____ 2. By changing what we are doing, we inevitably change what we think and feel.

_____ 3. Blaming others and making excuses for one's behavior lead to a cementing of one's identification with failure.

_____ 4. Involvement is the core of therapy, for without it there is no therapy.

_____ 5. Group leaders should not focus on misery and failures; rather, they should accentuate the members' strengths.

_____ 6. Group work should aim to change behavior rather than feelings or attitudes.

_____ 7. It is not the group leader's role to make value judgments for group members; rather, he or she should challenge them to evaluate their own behavior.

STAGES IN THE DEVELOPMENT OF THE REALITY THERAPY GROUP

Dimension	Initial Stage	Working Stage	Final Stage
Key developmental tasks and goals	First task is to create member-to-member relationships and a sense of involvement in the group. Leader-to-member relationships based on trust are essential. Major goal of initial stage is to get members to look at the degree to which current behavior is meeting their needs.	Focus is on present behavior, rather than feelings. Past is important only insofar as it influences present behavior. The central goal is to create a climate wherein members will learn to understand how their irresponsibility and poor choices have led to their personal problems; in this way members can establish "success" identity.	Specific plans for achieving desirable behavior patterns must be established. Although plans are crucial for behavioral change to occur, a noncritical therapeutic milieu must be created in order to give members the strength to carry out their plans.
Role of group leader and tasks	Group leader has the task of fostering involvement among the members; he or she encourages involvement by being active and involved with every member. Leader may question, ask others to make comments, and encourage interaction in the group. Modeling is crucial. Leader nudges members to look at what they are getting from their behavior.	Leader encourages members to evaluate their own behavior, asks members whether their behavior is meeting their needs, and firmly rejects excuses and rationalizations. Leader teaches members how to apply the basics of control theory to their lives. Counselor avoids labeling people with diagnostic categories.	Leader assists members in formulating realistic plans for change and creates a noncritical therapeutic climate that helps them believe that change is possible. Leader does not give up, even if members fail to carry out plans; he or she insists on finding a short-range plan that will lead to success.
Role of group members	Members concentrate on current behavior and problem areas. Focus may be on how each member attempts to gain love and feelings of self-worth and success. Members are expected to face their problems and to make plans to solve them. Making these plans for change begins early in the group.	Members evaluate own behavior and make value judgments about this behavior. They must understand what they are doing as well as what they are getting from this behavior. After they decide if they have what they want, members must decide for themselves if they are willing to change their patterns of behavior.	Realistic plans to change behavior are made and carried out. If members do not carry out their plans, they are expected to state when they will complete them. They are to accept responsibility for what they do and to make commitments.

Techniques	In keeping with the goal of establishing involvement, leader will encourage members to talk about any subjects of interest to them. An attempt is made to find out what members want from the group, and contracts are typically developed.	Confrontation; insistence on importance of evaluating behavior and making decisions; avoidance of punishment. Leader uses techniques of skillful questioning.	Contracts; behavioral strategies, such as role playing, behavior rehearsal, homework assignments, and so on; encouragement and support.
Questions to consider	Once you have established a relationship with members, you will want to focus on current behavior. In doing so, questions you may want to ask are: – What are you doing now? – What did you do this week? – What did you want to do differently this past week? – What stopped you from doing what you wanted to do? – What will you do tomorrow? If your members seem reluctant to accept the responsibility for their own problems, what might you do? How can you teach acceptance of responsibility? What use might you make of contracts? How would you help members establish clear and realistic goals? Would you focus exclusively on behavioral goals? Would you work with feelings and thoughts as well as current behavior?	A central task is to get members to look at what they are doing to decide whether their course of action is working. How can you challenge members in a nonjudgmental way to make an evaluation of their behavior? How can you avoid lecturing and imposing your values on members? How can you challenge members to make an honest evaluation if they seem resistant? What if the members cling to what you consider self-defeating ways of behaving? What do you see as your role in planning with members, checking with them about how well the plan is working, and making revisions in plans as needed? How can you use the group process in helping members make and follow through with their commitments?	How might you avoid giving up on certain members, even if they fail to meet their commitments? What might you do with members who do not seem willing to carry out short-range plans? What are some ways to use the group sessions to help members practice new behaviors that they will try out in daily situations? What methods might you employ to encourage members to practice outside the group what they are learning in the session? What are some ways to help members express and explore their fears of failing? How can you reinforce success and small gains? Can you think of ways to encourage members to take action, even though they feel defeated? What follow-up procedures might you use to assess the extent to which members make and maintain positive changes after a group?

Reactions: Summarize your reactions to the reality-therapy perspective on group developmental stages. What do you like *most?* *least?* What aspects of this approach would you incorporate in your leadership style?

_____ 8. Insight is *not* essential to produce change.

_____ 9. Unless clients are willing to accept responsibility for their behavior, they will not be able to change their behavior.

_____ 10. Group members are able to change when they accept that what they are doing, thinking, and feeling is not simply happening to them but that they are making choices.

Summary of Basic Assumptions and Key Concepts of the Reality-Therapy Approach to Groups

1. Reality therapy focuses on solving problems, on coping with the demands of reality in society, and on taking better control of one's life. By evaluating what we are doing and what we want, we are able to shape our destiny.

2. We perceive the world against the background of our needs rather the way it is in reality. We create our own inner world. We are not locked into any one mode of behavior, although we must behave in some way. Behavior is the attempt to control our perceptions of the external world to fit our internal and personal world.

3. Reality-therapy group leaders assist members with skillful questioning, which is aimed at getting them to assess what they want. Leaders assume a verbally active and directive role in the group. Their main task is to encourage the members to face reality and make value judgments about their behavior. Thus, behavior is the focus, rather than insight. Leaders tend to focus on the strengths and potentials of members rather than failures. This is done by challenging members to look at their unused potential and to move toward creating a success identity and more effective control.

4. Group leaders using reality therapy stress what members can do now to change their behavior: make a commitment to change, develop a plan for action, and follow through. Thus, they do not explore the past, and they do not accept any excuses for the failure of members to follow through with their commitments.

5. The practice of reality therapy involves two major components: (1) the counseling environment and (2) specific procedures that lead to changes in behavior. A great deal of emphasis is placed on creating a supportive environment that allows clients to change. Through a process of skillful questioning, leaders help members recognize, define, and refine how they wish to meet their needs. Members explore what they want, what they have, and what they are not getting. Leaders function by holding a mirror before the members and asking "What do you see for yourself now and in the future?"

Exercises and Activities for Reality Therapy in Groups

Rationale

Reality therapy is a practical approach with many uses and applications to a variety of types of groups. As you review the basic concepts and principles of control theory, think about ways to translate them into your practice with different kinds of groups. Also, reflect on how you could apply control theory to help you get what you want and to gain more effective control of your own life. Some of the following exercises, activities, and questions can be used on your own, and others can be used in small groups. After you have worked with this material and answered the questions, you will be in a better position to know which of these ideas you might want to employ in the groups you lead or will lead.

Exercises

1. *Are you meeting your needs?* Control theory holds that total behavior is purposeful, that it originates from within the individual rather than from external sources, and that psychological needs are powerful motivating forces. Control theory also contends that we develop pictures in our head (or an inner picture album) of specific wants. Our inner picture makes up our ideal world, or the way we want life to be. Our pictures determine our life. We are motivated to mold the external world to match the ever-changing inner world. Discuss the ways in which your psychological needs are being met, as well as how you see them influencing your daily behavior. Arrange the following four needs in the order of priority to you. As you review these needs, attempt to identify what you consider to be your key strengths.

    a. *Belonging.* What do you do to meet your needs for involvement with others? In what ways do you feel a sense of belonging?

    b. *Power.* When do you feel a sense of power? In what areas of your life do you feel most competent? When do you feel recognized?

    c. *Freedom.* To what degree do you feel that you are in charge of your life and that you are moving in the direction that you want?

    d. *Fun.* What activities do you do for fun? Do you have as much fun as you would like?

2. *Choosing your total behavior.* Control theory is based on the assumption that we choose our total behavior, which is composed of the interrelated elements of *doing, thinking, feeling,* and *physiology.* In our attempt to gain more effective control, we behave in the world to get the picture we want at the time. Every total behavior is our best attempt to get what we want. Considering this set of basic assumptions, discuss the following questions as they apply to you in your group.

    a. What experiences have you had that either support or reject the notion that you have almost complete ability to change what you are doing and some ability to change what you are thinking? Do you find it is easier to change what you are doing and thinking rather than what you are feeling?

    b. To what extent do you find that when you begin to act differently, that you also change what you are thinking and feeling? Can you provide any personal examples?

    c. Glasser contends that it is inaccurate to speak of being depressed, having a headache, or being anxious. Instead, he says that these are action states that we are choosing. Thus, it is more accurate to say that we are *depressing, headaching,* and *anxietying.* In your group provide examples of states that you think you have some control over. Are you willing to assume responsibility for these states? Or do you think that some of your behaviors (actions, thoughts, feelings, physiology) are beyond your control?

3. *"Success" and "failure" identities.*

    a. How does what you say about yourself affect the way people view and treat you? What self-fulfilling prophecies do you subject yourself to? In what ways do you set yourself up for success or failure?

    b. If your parents were to describe you in terms of a success/failure identity, what might they say about you? What do you imagine your best friend would say? If you are in a group now, how do you think other members might perceive you?

c. Is there a difference between the way you see yourself now and the way you'd like to be? If so, what changes would you like to make? In what ways do you restrict your possibilities by rigidly adhering to fixed notions that do not allow for change? Do you tell yourself that you can't be other than you are—that you can't change?

4. *Value judgment and self-evaluation.* A central procedure in reality therapy consists of asking members to determine whether they are getting what they want and whether their behavior is working for them. Spend some time thinking about how making an evaluation of your behavior could benefit you.

   a. As you review your behavior on a given day, what would you most want to change about yourself? Are there any specific actions or thoughts that you would like to change because you determine that they are not working for you? To what degree do you think that you are getting what you want?

   b. What are some values that are important to you? What difficulties do you, as a group leader, predict that you'll have as a result of value clashes with group members? What clients would you have difficulty working with in a group because of a divergence in philosophy, lifestyle, and value system?

5. *Involvement.* Reality therapy stresses the importance of involvement (or a spirit of caring) as the foundation for the group process. Ask yourself:

   a. If you are in a group now, to what degree do you experience a sense of involvement with the leader and the other members?

   b. Do you think the group leader should become involved with the participants? Why or why not? How would you involve yourself in your groups? With what clients would you most easily become involved? With what people would it be difficult for you to become involved?

6. *Developing a plan for change.*

   a. Think about a particular behavior that you want to change and are willing to change. If you are in a group at this time, work out a specific plan that will lead to change. Discuss the details of the plan with those in your group. One of the best ways to understand the process of formulating personal plans is to develop such a plan yourself.

   b. What commitments would you, as a leader, expect from those who participated in your groups? What methods would you use to assist them in formulating specific action plans? How do you imagine that you'd handle participants who continually made plans but then returned to the group without having followed through on most of them?

   c. How would you, as a group member, deal with group members who talked about wanting to change but refused to make any concrete plans to put into action outside the group? Perhaps they would insist that they had never been able to make plans. What would you tell them?

7. *Role-playing activity with involuntary group members.* In your class/group discuss some reality-therapy strategies that you might use if you were leading or co-leading an involuntary group. After this discussion each of the members can assume the identity of an involuntary group member and then role-play this person in your group. Two students can function as co-leaders and demonstrate how you might work with such a group. Attempt to keep within the reality-therapy perspective. Allow enough time before the end of the session for processing. What was it like to lead this group by staying within the boundaries of this approach? What was the experience like for those who role-played an involuntary client?

8. *Role-playing activity for a particular age group.* This is an activity that you can do in your group or in a small group within the large class. Decide on a particular age group—children, adolescents, the elderly—and think of a particular focus for the group. For example, you might have a group for children who are coping with divorce, a group for adolescents who want to explore social and personal problems they are facing, or a group for the elderly who are in a day-care facility. Each person role-plays a particular individual in the chosen group. Identify a concern that you think you have empathy for and could get involved with through role playing. Two members can volunteer to be the co-leaders using a reality-therapy orientation. Apply what you know of control theory and the kinds of interventions made in reality therapy to leading this group. After the session devote time to processing the possible advantages and disadvantages of working with this type of group with this approach.

9. *Role-playing activity with a specific value issue.* Think about a concern of a group member that might pose difficulties for you as a group leader. It would be helpful to identify a member's value conflict that you think would challenge you to be objective or helpful. Below are specific value issues that members are likely to present.

   a. The client is an adolescent girl who is struggling with whether to have an abortion.

   b. The client is having difficulty in accepting the religion that he was brought up with, yet he hesitates to leave the religion because of his fears and guilt feelings.

   c. The client discloses that he is having an affair and is not certain whether he wants to remain married and keep the affair going or leave his wife for the other woman.

   d. The client is a member of an ethnic group that values loyalty to one's family. This woman is contemplating leaving her husband because of her deep dissatisfaction with what she refers to as a "dead-end relationship." What mainly stops her are "internal voices" that remind her that she would bring shame to her entire family if she were to divorce.

   These are a few examples of potential value conflicts that could arise in a group. Think of your own illustrations of cases that you might find most difficult to deal with in group counseling. As a role-playing activity, assume the personality of the client who you think would be the most challenging for you to work with, and stay with this characterization. Again, two members can volunteer to co-lead this reality-therapy group. Remember that within this framework the group leader would not make decisions for these clients but would assist them in evaluating their own behavior to determine what they want to do. After the session discuss what you learned by assuming a particular client's identity and talk about what it was like to work in this approach.

10. *Personal critique of the reality-therapy approach to groups.*

    a. For what populations do you think reality therapy is most appropriate?

    b. What are the basic ideas and practices of this approach that you are most inclined to include in your work with groups?

    c. In the context of cultural diversity, what do you consider to be the major assets and limitations of employing reality-therapy techniques? What specific aspects of this approach might be most useful in working with minority and ethnic clients?

    d. What possibilities can you think of for creative combinations between reality therapy and some of the other approaches that you have studied? Discuss what elements of other approaches that you might be inclined to incorporate in a reality-therapy perspective.

    e. How would it be for you to practice almost exclusively within this approach? What do you imagine it would be like for you to be a member of a reality-therapy group?

PART

III
APPLICATION
AND INTEGRATION

16

Illustration of a Group in Action: Various Perspectives

Guidelines for Critiquing Various Approaches to Group Therapy

The textbook's illustration of a group in action is designed to give you a general picture of how different group-counseling approaches could be applied to the same group. Thus, it gives you practical examples of the advantages and disadvantages of each approach. In your class or group, using the following questions as a guide, discuss what aspects you like best (and least) about each approach as it was presented in the textbook illustration. Then explore the ways to integrate several approaches in your own leadership style—to selectively borrow concepts and procedures from all of the therapies—and to begin developing your own theory of group counseling.

Using the Psychoanalytic Approach

1. How would group members' resistance be explained? How might resistance be handled by the leader?

2. How could the leader work with any strong feelings that the members directed against him or her?

3. What would the group leader primarily focus on in this group?

4. At what stage of a group's development do you think psychoanalytic concepts and techniques are most suitable? What would you most want to incorporate in your style from this approach?

Using the Adlerian Approach

1. How would an Adlerian go about getting early recollections from members, and how would these memories be used in the group?

2. What possibilities can you see in using the group as a way to re-create the original family of

the members? What are some ways in which work with the family constellation could be included in a group context?

3. Adlerians are interested in the personal goals of members, including a focus on what they are working toward and what kind of life they want. Applied to the group described in the chapter, how might a leader work with member goals?

4. At what stage of a group's development do you think Adlerian concepts and techniques are most appropriate? What concepts and techniques would you want to draw from in this approach?

Using Psychodrama

1. How could the group leader "warm up" the group? (Would you use any of these techniques in your group work?)

2. What value would the group leader place on reenacting past events or enacting anticipated situations? (What do psychodrama and the psychoanalytic approach have in common? How do they differ?)

3. How could the group leader work with relationship conflicts?

4. At what stage of a group's development would psychodramatic procedures be most effective? What do you want to take from this approach?

Using the Existential Approach

1. How might the theme "I'm alive, but I feel dead" be explained and dealt with?

2. How would the group leader describe this group and explain the occurrences in it, as opposed to the description of a group leader using the psychoanalytic approach?

3. How could the group leader deal with group members who found little meaning in life and who expressed suicidal thoughts? (How would you deal with these issues as a group leader?)

4. At what stage of a group's development would this approach be most appropriate?

Using the Person-Centered Approach

1. How would the leader attempt to create trust?

2. How could the group leader work with a member who expressed problems with loneliness?

3. How could the leader provide more direction? (Do you think this group or any particular members in it *need* more direction and structure than is illustrated?)

4. At what stage of a group's development might this approach be of the most value? What do you want to draw on from the approach?

Using the Gestalt Approach

1. How might the group leader work with the members of this group, as contrasted with the way a person-centered group leader would work?

2. If a member in this group wanted to work on a dream that related to emptiness, how would the leader carry this out?

3. Would the group leader use many action-oriented therapeutic techniques? Why or why not?

4. At what stage of a group's development do you see Gestalt as being most useful and appropriate?

Using Transactional Analysis

1. How would the TA leader—as opposed to a psychoanalytic leader—work with a member's drinking problem?

2. Contracts will be made between the leader and the members. How do you think contracts will work in this group?

3. What role would examining old decisions and making new ones play in this group's work?

4. At what stage of a group's development do you think TA is most useful? What concepts and techniques do you want to use from TA?

Using the Behavioral Approach

1. How would the group leader begin the group? (What are the typical steps and sequences in the behavioral group?)

2. How would the leader work with this group, as contrasted with a psychoanalytic leader? an existential leader? a Gestalt leader?

3. How could the group leader work with a member who is very unassertive? (How would *you* work with such a problem?)

4. At what stage of a group would behavioral methods be most appropriate? Which of these methods are you most likely to use in your leading?

Using the Rational-Emotive Approach

1. The techniques employed in group work are directive and confrontational. Would you be comfortable using these techniques in your own group?

2. How might the leader deal with the member who fears rejection? (How would this tactic differ from what the person-centered therapist would do?)

3. How could the leader deal with the member with a marriage problem? (How would this intervention differ from what an RET therapist would do? from what a leader using psychodrama would do?)

4. At what stage in a group would RET be most appropriate? What might you take from RET and use in your style of leading?

Using Reality Therapy

1. How would the group leader respond to a member who has blamed his past for his current problems?

2. How could the leader get members to evaluate their current behavior?

3. In what ways would the reality-therapy leader assist members in formulating a plan for action? How is what one is doing in the present related to making plans for change and committing oneself to this program?

4. At what stage in the group's development would reality therapy be most useful?

17

Comparisons, Contrasts, and Integration

Questions for Discussion and Evaluation

Perspectives on Goals for Group Counseling

1. How does the theoretical orientation of a group practitioner influence the group's goals and the direction it takes? How can a leader's values and beliefs influence the direction of the group?

2. In view of the many differences among the various theoretical approaches to group therapy, how is a common ground possible among behavioral-oriented groups and experiential- and relationship-oriented groups? How can long-range goals and concrete short-term goals be integrated into group practice?

3. As a group leader, what value would you place on the freedom of members to select personal goals? How would you bring the members' goals and the goals you have for the group into agreement? What problems can you foresee if these goals do not agree?

4. How do a group's goals relate to its type of membership?

5. Consult the overview chart of goals for group counseling in the textbook. Decide which approaches come closest to your thinking with respect to goals. Which model(s) do you find least helpful in clarifying your own vision of the purpose of a group? As you review the models, determine which goals you'd choose to incorporate in your own counseling.

Role and Function of the Group Leader

1. In the text, review the chart that summarizes the role and function of the group leader in the various theoretical approaches. What do you see as your specific roles and functions in leading a group? To what degree does your role depend on the stage of development of your group?

2. If your group is characterized by cultural diversity, what do you see as your role in

encouraging members to explore their feelings about their similarities and differences? What is your role in helping members take their cultural heritage and values into account as they explore their concerns and make decisions about their lives?

3. If you were asked in a job interview to briefly describe what you considered your central role as a group leader to be, what would you say?

Group Leader's Use of Techniques

1. Review the chart in the textbook on techniques that flow from each of the theories. Which techniques are you most inclined to employ? How would your selection of techniques depend on the kind of group you were leading? How would you adapt your techniques to fit the needs of culturally diverse populations? What techniques seem to be most congruent with your personality and leadership style?

2. What techniques are you most likely to use at each of the stages of a group's development? What techniques are you inclined to use in opening a group session? in closing a group session? in assisting members to evaluate their progress?

3. What is the purpose of techniques in groups? When do techniques most enhance group process? When might their use interfere with the progress of a group? What are your ideas evaluating the effectiveness of the techniques that you introduce?

The Issue of Structuring and the Division of Responsibility

1. It is clear that a group leader will provide *structure* for the group. What is *not* predetermined is the *degree* and *kind* of structure he or she provides. The group could range from being extremely unstructured (the person-centered group) to being highly structured and directive (the behavioral group). Review the chart in the textbook on degree of structuring and division of responsibility. Which theories come closest to your view? Why? What theories do you disagree with? Why? How could you combine some of these different approaches to structuring a group? How can these models stimulate your thinking regarding what type and degree of structuring you want to provide a group? How does structuring relate to the group's stage of development?

2. *The division of responsibility*, like structuring, can differ widely according to the theoretical approach used in a group. Some therapies place primary responsibility on the leader for the direction and outcome of the group. Other therapies give primary responsibility to the group members and tend to downplay the role of the leader. What is your position?

3. The group leader must always maintain a balance between taking on too much responsibility for the group and denying any responsibility for its direction. What problems do you foresee for a group if the leader assumes either too much or not enough responsibility?

4. Review the chart in the textbook on the division of responsibility, and then decide what approaches provide you with the most insight on this issue.

Theories Applied to Multicultural Group Counseling

1. If your groups are culturally diverse, which theoretical approaches would you find most useful in understanding the members? Identify several approaches that provide you with a conceptual framework and methods that would be helpful in addressing ethnic and cultural concerns.

2. What group practices do you think might pose problems for some clients because of their cultural background? One example is the expectation that clients will disclose here-and-now feelings as they emerge within a group. Some people have been culturally conditioned to hide their feelings and, thus, are likely to have difficulty with self-disclosure. Shame may be associated with showing feelings, especially outside of one's family setting. What help could you provide to those members who have trouble participating in your group because of a conflict between the group norms and their cultural values.

3. What do you consider to be a few of the major limitations of the theories in working with a multicultural population? Which particular approach do you see as being the most limited in addressing ethnic and cultural variables in a group?

Toward a Synthesis of Theories Applied to Practice

Review the sections of the chapter in the textbook that deal with developing an *integrated eclectic model* of group counseling. Strive to begin developing your own synthesis of theories applied to groups at the various stages of development. I suggest that you use the questions below as the basis for discussion in small groups. With your fellow students, think of ways to develop a conceptual framework that can account for the factors of cognition, emotion, and behavior. Also, focus on various theoretical approaches that you'd probably draw on at each of the stages in the life history of a group. Strive for a blending and an integration of theories that will provide you with a cognitive map to explain what goes on in a group as it evolves.

1. What general *group-process goals* would guide your interventions at the initial, transition, working, and final stages of a group? How might the goals for a group differ with respect to the period of development?

2. How would you describe your major *role and functions* at each of the stages of a group? What changes, if any, do you see in your leadership functions at the various phases?

3. What kind of *structuring* do you most want to provide at each of the phases of a group's development? How would you describe the division of responsibility (between you as leader and the members) at each of the stages?

4. In terms of *techniques* in the facilitation of group process at the various phases of development, what possible integration can you come up with? How can you combine theories and techniques to work on the three levels of thinking/feeling/doing? (For example, can you think of ways to combine experiential techniques with cognitive and behavioral methods? What ways might you blend Gestalt or psychodramatic methods with RET or behavioral techniques?)

5. During the *pregroup* stage how could you draw on those approaches that stress *therapeutic contracts*? How might you help members formulate a contract during the screening and orientation interview?

6. During the *initial* stage what aspects of the relationship-oriented approaches (especially the existential and person-centered approaches) could you use as a basis for building trust among the members and between yourself and the members? How might you look to the behavioral approaches in assisting members to develop specific personal goals?

7. During the *transition* stage how might you understand resistance from a psychoanalytic and an Adlerian perspective? How could you work with resistance by using the group as a way to re-create the members' original family? Can you think of theories you could draw on that would help you work with members from a thinking/feeling/behaving perspective when a group is in transition?

8. During the *working* stage what integration of theoretical perspectives will allow you to consider the thinking/feeling/behaving dimensions? How much emphasis would you be inclined to place on the expression of emotion? How much focus would you place on what members are thinking and how their cognitions influence their behavior? What are some examples of techniques you'd employ to work on a behavioral level? Can you think of ways in which you might use role playing, behavior rehearsal, and feedback? What ways can you think of to promote interaction among the members? How could you link the work of several members? What are some ways to develop themes in a group that many members are able to work with at the same time?

9. During the *final* stage how could you borrow strategies from the cognitive-behavioral therapies to help members consolidate their learning and apply it to life outside of the group? What are some ways in which you might help members practice new learning? What are some ways of teaching members how to create support systems once they leave a group?

10. At the *postgroup* stage how could you apply behavioral strategies for accountability and evaluation purposes? What specific follow-up procedures would you want for the groups you lead?

Note: Now that you have addressed the questions above, attempt to develop your own questions on the applications of theory to group practice, and look toward your own personal synthesis. Explain how you see groups from a developmental perspective, giving emphasis to those theories that most help you understand how groups function.

Comprehension Check and General Test

The following test is designed to help you assess your understanding of basic concepts of the textbook. Take it toward the end of the semester to determine what areas may still need further study. If you have the time, consider outlining the essay questions given after the objective test. For your convenience, a scoring sheet is given after the test. Another set of questions, similar in format and content, is available to instructors.

This test will help prepare you for an objective test if such a test is given as a part of your course. Select the *one best* answer.

Multiple-Choice Items

_____ 1. A major difference between group therapy and group counseling lies
   a. in their techniques.
   b. in the group process.
   c. in the goals for the group.

_____ 2. All of the following are true of structured groups except for one.
   a. They impart information.
   b. They teach people how to solve problems.
   c. They help clients learn to create their own support systems outside of the group.
   d. They tend to be long term.

_____ 3. All of the following are similarities between self-help groups and therapy groups except for one.
   a. Both are led by qualified professionals.
   b. Both encourage support and stress the value of affiliation.
   c. Both aim for behavioral change.
   d. Both make use of the group process.

_____ 4. In self-help groups the focus tends to be on
   a. discussing the external causes of members' problems.

b. developing strategies to deal with environmental pressures and barriers.

c. stressing a common identity based on a common life situation.

d. all of the above.

_____ 5. If you are involved in group work with culturally diverse populations, it will be important for you to

a. be an expert on each of the populations.

b. accept the challenge of modifying your strategies to meet the unique needs of the members.

c. be of the same ethnic background as the members in your group.

d. do all of the above.

_____ 6. Which of the following is an advantage of group work with multicultural populations?

a. Members can gain much from the power and strength of collective group feedback.

b. Modeling operates in groups.

c. In groups, people learn that they are not alone in their struggles.

d. Cross-cultural universality often exists in such groups.

e. All of the above are advantages.

_____ 7. A limitation of group work in a multicultural context is

a. that groups have been proved ineffective in working with ethnic clients.

b. that many ethnic clients consider it shameful to talk about their personal problems in front of others.

c. that ethnic clients will not be able to develop trust in a group setting.

d. that there is no basis for sharing common struggles or common pain.

_____ 8. All of the following are examples of Western values except for one.

a. interdependence

b. freedom

c. responsibility

d. achievement

_____ 9. Assume that you are leading a group and a particular ethnic client tends to be very quiet. Which of the following might best explain this silence?

a. This is surely a sign of a resistant client.

b. This is evidence that this client does not want to be in the group.

c. The silence may indicate politeness and a sense of respect.

d. This hesitation is best interpreted as a stubborn refusal to be open.

e. This member should be asked to leave the group.

_____ 10. If you are intending to form a group composed of culturally diverse members, it would be important to

a. prepare the clients for the group experience.

b. have a general understanding of the cultural values of your clients.

c. develop patience in accepting differences in behavior.

d. help members clearly identify why they are in a group.

e. do all of the above.

_____ 11. Which of the following captures the essence of informed consent?

a. having members sign a contract before joining a group

b. telling members in some detail about the nature and purpose of the group

c. having members decide on all of the activities of the group

d. making sure that groups will always be composed of voluntary members

_____ 12. The principle of informed consent applies to

a. voluntary groups only.

b. involuntary groups only.

c. both voluntary and involuntary groups.

13. On the matter of coercion and pressure in a group, members should know that
    a. some pressure is to be expected as part of group process.
    b. they have a right to be protected against undue pressure.
    c. coercion to make acceptable decisions may be a part of group procedure.
    d. they may well be pressured to participate in threatening nonverbal exercises.
    e. both (a) and (b) are true.

14. On the issue of psychological risks in groups, what can be safely said?
    a. In a well-designed group, there are really no psychological risks.
    b. Since groups can be catalysts for change, they also contain risks.
    c. Members can be given guarantees that a group will not involve risks.
    d. There are risks only when members are not properly screened.

15. What kind of clinical practice is endorsed by the ASGW as a means of gaining supervised experience in group work?
    a. critiquing group tapes
    b. co-leading groups with supervision
    c. participating as a member in a group
    d. observing group-counseling sessions
    e. all of the above

16. A training group for beginning leaders primarily focuses on
    a. problems the group leaders are having in their personal lives.
    b. the skills necessary for effective intervention.
    c. a discussion of theories of group counseling.
    d. learning structured techniques and exercises for most problems that might arise within a group.

17. Which of the following would *not* be considered one of a group member's rights?
    a. the right to expect protection from verbal or physical assaults
    b. the right to expect complete confidentiality
    c. the right to know the leader's qualifications
    d. the right to help from the group leader in developing personal goals
    e. the right to expect freedom from undue group pressure

18. Regarding the issue of freedom of exit, which is the recommended course of action?
    a. Members should be able to leave at any time they wish without any explanation.
    b. Members should never be allowed to leave a group once they being.
    c. Members who are thinking of leaving should bring the issue up for discussion in the session.
    d. Members should bring up the issue of leaving privately with the leader, the group, or both.
    e. Two of the above are true.

19. Regarding the right to confidentiality, which statement is false?
    a. Confidentiality is one of the key norms of behavior in a group.
    b. Confidentiality is often on the minds of people when they initially join a group.
    c. Members who are in an involuntary group have no rights to confidentiality.
    d. It is a good practice to remind participants from time to time of the danger of inadvertently revealing confidences.

20. The key to a group leader's avoiding a malpractice suit consists of maintaining
    a. reasonable practices.
    b. ordinary practices.
    c. prudent practices.
    d. all of the above.
    e. none of the above.

_____ 21. Which is the correct sequence of the stages of a group?
   a. transition, initial, working, consolidation
   b. initial, transition, consolidation, working
   c. initial, transition, working, consolidation
   d. transition, initial, consolidation, working

_____ 22. Which stage is characterized by dealing with conflict, defensiveness, and resistance?
   a. working stage
   b. transition stage
   c. consolidation stage
   d. initial stage

_____ 23. Inclusion and identity are the primary tasks of which stage of a group?
   a. initial stage
   b. transition stage
   c. working stage
   d. final stage

_____ 24. Teaching participants some general guidelines of group functioning, developing group norms, and assisting members to express their fears and expectations are all group leadership functions during the
   a. working stage.
   b. transition stage.
   c. initial and exploration phase.
   d. consolidation phase.

_____ 25. Which stage is generally characterized by increased anxiety and defensiveness?
   a. initial stage
   b. transition stage
   c. working stage
   d. final stage

_____ 26. Cohesion and productivity are most closely associated with the
   a. working stage.
   b. transition stage.
   c. initial and exploration phase.
   d. consolidation phase.

_____ 27. Conflict and struggle for control are most likely to appear in the
   a. working stage.
   b. transition stage.
   c. initial and exploration phase.
   d. consolidation phase.

_____ 28. Resistance in a group can be seen as
   a. inevitable.
   b. material for productive exploration.
   c. a bad attitude on the part of the member.
   d. something that should be avoided at all costs.
   e. both (a) and (b).

_____ 29. When attempting to organize and begin a group in an agency, it is important to
   a. be aware of the politics involved in the setting in which you work.
   b. give up the idea if no one else on the staff seems excited about it.
   c. expect the support and encouragement of your co-workers.
   d. do all of the above.

_____ 30. When working with involuntary group members, it is important to
    a. expect that they will figure out on their own the best way to participate.
    b. discuss with them ways to use the time beneficially.
    d. insist that they participate.
    e. assume that they will understand the basic group procedures after being there for a few sessions.

True/False Items

_____ 31. Structured groups, or groups characterized by some central theme, have recently declined in popularity.

_____ 32. Structured groups are often based on a learning-theory model and use behavioral procedures.

_____ 33. The terms _self-help group_ and _support group_ are often used interchangeably.

_____ 34. Essentially, self-help groups and therapy groups have the same goals.

_____ 35. Self-help groups often focus on exploring external causes of member problems as well as developing strategies to deal with environmental pressures and barriers.

_____ 36. The literature dealing with multicultural counseling indicates that ethnic and minority clients are making full use of mental-health services.

_____ 37. Group leaders may encounter resistance from some ethnic or minority clients because they are using traditional White, middle-class values to interpret these clients' experiences.

_____ 38. An advantage of group work with ethnic clients is that members can gain from the power and strength of collective group feedback.

_____ 39. A disadvantage of group work with ethnic clients is their reluctance to disclose personal material or to share family secrets.

_____ 40. If an ethnic client displays silence in a group, this behavior is most probably a sign of resistance.

_____ 41. It is best not to inform clients of their rights as members before they join a group, for this generally reduces their commitment to work.

_____ 42. It is clearly unethical to form groups composed of involuntary members.

_____ 43. It is a good practice to remind participants from time to time of the danger of inadvertently breaking confidentiality.

_____ 44. One way to establish trust is to reassure members that whatever they disclose in a session will never go outside of the group.

_____ 45. It is realistic to assume that adequately led groups, by their very nature, eliminate psychological risks to the participants.

_____ 46. It is unwise to forewarn participants of the psychological risks of being in a group, for this is likely to create a tense climate and lead to extreme caution.

_____ 47. It is important that group leaders be clear about their own values and express them openly when it is relevant and appropriate to the work of the group.

_____ 48. As a group counselor you may face the need in a malpractice action to justify the techniques you have used.

_____ 49. Group leaders who possess personal power generally meet their needs at the expense of the members and are therefore unethical.

_____ 50. Research findings on leader self-disclosure clearly indicate that the more leaders disclose of their personal lives, the more their groups become self-directed and cohesive.

Definition Items

Select the group-leadership skill that is described by each phrase.

_____ 51. Identifying with clients by assuming their internal frames of reference.
    a. sympathizing
    b. empathizing
    c. facilitating
    d. reflecting
    e. none of the above

_____ 52. Expressing concrete and honest reactions based on observation of members' behavior.
    a. evaluating
    b. initiating
    c. clarifying
    d. interpreting
    e. giving feedback

_____ 53. Attending to verbal and nonverbal aspects of communication without judging or evaluating.
    a. interpreting
    b. reflecting feelings
    c. active listening
    d. facilitating
    e. empathizing

_____ 54. Demonstrating desired behavior through actions.
    a. modeling
    b. clarifying
    c. facilitating
    d. evaluating
    e. none of the above

_____ 55. Challenging participants to look at discrepancies between their words and actions, or verbal and nonverbal communication.
    a. confronting
    b. suggesting
    c. clarifying
    d. interpreting
    e. initiating

_____ 56. Revealing one's reactions to here-and-now events in the group.
    a. restating
    b. empathizing
    c. confronting
    d. disclosing oneself
    e. linking

_____ 57. Promoting member-to-member interactions rather than focusing on member-to-leader interactions.
   a. summarizing
   b. linking
   c. suggesting
   d. reflecting feelings
   e. questioning

_____ 58. Safeguarding members from unnecessary psychological risks in the group.
   a. modeling
   b. linking
   c. goal setting
   d. interpreting
   e. protecting

_____ 59. Preparing a group to close a session or end its existence.
   a. restating
   b. terminating
   c. summarizing
   d. evaluating
   e. questioning

_____ 60. Planning specific goals for the group process and helping participants define concrete personal issues as the focus of work.
   a. supporting
   b. clarifying
   c. facilitating
   d. goal setting
   e. suggesting

Conceptual Items

Items 61 through 85 present a series of related concepts or techniques pertaining to one therapeutic approach. _One item in the series of five does not fit with the other four items._ Identify the word or phrase that does not fit.

_____ 61. (a) life stages, (b) developmental crises, (c) psychosocial stages, (d) stress inoculation, (e) critical tasks

_____ 62. (a) fictional finalism, (b) basic mistakes, (c) A-B-C theory, (d) social interest, (e) style of life

_____ 63. (a) playing the projection, (b) the rehearsal experiment, (c) family modeling, (d) staying with the feeling, (e) making the rounds

_____ 64. (a) style of life, (b) openness to experience, (c) self-trust, (d) internal source of evaluation, (e) willingness to continue growing

_____ 65. (a) behavior therapy, (b) mistaken goals, (c) private logic, (d) early recollections, (e) family constellation

_____ 66. (a) congruence, (b) redecision, (c) internal source of evaluation, (d) unconditional positive regard, (e) accurate empathic understanding

_____ 67. (a) value judgments, (b) plan for action, (c) commitment, (d) unconditional positive regard, (e) success identity

_____ 68. (a) A-B-C theory, (b) irrational beliefs, (c) control theory, (d) cognitive restructuring, (e) self-defeating thought patterns

_____ 69. (a) present-centered awareness, (b) the concept of the now, (c) unfinished business, (d) accurate empathic understanding, (e) bringing the past into the here-and-now

_____ 70. (a) relaxation training, (b) the dialogue experiment, (c) staying with the feeling, (d) reversal technique, (e) present-centered dream work

_____ 71. (a) injunctions, (b) existential anxiety, (c) early decisions, (d) games, (e) redecisions

_____ 72. (a) early recollections, (b) strokes, (c) life scripts, (d) games, (e) early decisions

_____ 73. (a) social-skills training, (b) cognitive restructuring, (c) modeling methods, (d) assertiveness training, (e) analysis of transference

_____ 74. (a) the dialogue experiment, (b) cognitive restructuring, (c) exaggeration experiment, (d) rehearsal experiment, (e) making the rounds

_____ 75. (a) games, (b) rackets, (c) scripting, (d) catharsis, (e) Parent, Adult, Child

_____ 76. (a) layers of neurosis, (b) unfinished business, (c) ego states, (d) contact and resistance to contact, (e) energy and blocks to energy

_____ 77. (a) modeling, (b) coaching, (c) imitation, (d) social learning, (e) observational learning

_____ 78. (a) multimodal therapy, (b) BASIC ID, (c) technical eclecticism, (d) therapeutic flexibility and versatility, (e) control theory

_____ 79. (a) Gestalt experiments, (b) assertiveness training, (c) stress-management training, (d) social-skill training, (e) self-directed behavior

_____ 80. (a) total behavior, (b) control theory, (c) existential/phenomenological orientation, (d) redecisional therapy, (e) success identity

_____ 81. (a) establishing the relationship, (b) exploring the individual's dynamics, (c) working through transference neurosis, (d) encouraging insight, (e) helping with reorientation

_____ 82. (a) experiential therapy, (b) existential therapy, (c) person-centered therapy, (d) Gestalt therapy, (e) psychoanalytic therapy

_____ 83. (a) disputation of irrational beliefs, (b) cognitive homework, (c) rational-emotive imagery, (d) shame-attacking exercises, (e) dialogue experiment

_____ 84. (a) I/Thou relationship, (b) life scripts, (c) redecisions, (d) injunctions and early decisions, (e) strokes

_____ 85. (a) reexperiencing one's past, (b) developing an action plan, (c) getting a commitment, (d) refusing to accept excuses, (e) refusing to use punishment

Multiple-Choice Items

_____ 86. Many analytically oriented group therapists have a leadership style that is characterized by
    a. objectivity, warm detachment, and relative anonymity.
    b. objectivity, aloofness, and strict anonymity.

    c. subjectivity, mutuality, and self-disclosure.
    d. rationality, impersonality, and coolness.

87. Adler stressed
    a. the value of transference for group therapy.
    b. the purposeful nature of behavior.
    c. the role of biological determinants of behavior.
    d. total behavior as a concept of control theory.
    e. none of the above.

88. Psychodrama was developed by
    a. Fritz Perls.
    b. Carl Rogers.
    c. J. L. Moreno.
    d. William Glasser.
    e. Albert Ellis.

89. The function of the existential group leader is
    a. to understand the member's subjective world.
    b. to explore the member's past history.
    c. to challenge each member to discover alternatives.
    d. two of the above.

90. The congruence of a group leader implies
    a. empathy.
    b. immediacy.
    c. genuineness.
    d. unconditional positive regard.
    e. none of the above.

91. Which of the following is *not* a key concept of the Gestalt group?
    a. awareness
    b. unfinished business
    c. understanding one's irrational beliefs
    d. here-and-now focus
    e. dealing with the impasse

92. The founder of transactional analysis is
    a. Robert Goulding.
    b. Eric Berne.
    c. J. L. Moreno.
    d. William Glasser.
    e. Albert Bandura.

93. Which of the following techniques is not considered a behavioral technique?
    a. self-instruction
    b. the dialogue technique
    c. cognitive restructuring
    d. self-reinforcement
    e. coaching

94. RET methodology includes all of the following procedures except
    a. confrontation.
    b. logical analysis.
    c. analysis of one's life script.
    d. counterpropaganda.
    e. behavioral methods.

_____ 95. Which of the following is not a key concept of reality therapy?
   a. Members must make commitments.
   b. Members focus on early childhood issues.
   c. Members make value judgments of their behavior.
   d. Members focus on the present, not the past.
   e. Members look at ways in which they are choosing their total behavior.

_____ 96. In an analytic group free association might be used for
   a. working on dreams.
   b. encouraging spontaneity among members.
   c. promoting interaction between members.
   d. getting at unconscious material.
   e. all of the above.

_____ 97. All of the following are key concepts underlying the Adlerian group except for one.
   a. teleology
   b. social interest
   c. creativity and choice
   d. developing a lifestyle
   e. A-B-C theory of personality

_____ 98. Which of the following techniques is least likely to be used in psychodrama?
   a. script analysis
   b. doubling
   c. future projection
   d. role reversal
   e. soliloquy

_____ 99. In an existential group which technique would be considered essential?
   a. role playing
   b. rational-emotive imagery
   c. homework
   d. dream analysis
   e. none of the above

_____ 100. The term that best captures the role and function of a person-centered group counselor is
   a. teacher.
   b. facilitator.
   c. expert.
   d. companion.

_____ 101. Which of the following is generally _not_ a technique used in Gestalt groups?
   a. experiments with dialogues
   b. making the rounds
   c. teaching rational thinking
   d. working with dreams
   e. focusing on nonverbal communication

_____ 102. Which of the following is _not_ a key concept of TA groups?
   a. lifestyle assessment
   b. analysis of ego states
   c. strokes
   d. script analysis
   e. games

_____ 103. During the initial stage of a behavioral group the concern of the group leader is
   a. to identify problematic behavior.

b. to develop baseline data.

c. to teach members about the group process.

d. to conduct an assessment of each member's current behavior.

e. to do all of the above.

_____ 104. In an RET group, role playing involves

a. a catharsis.

b. a cognitive restructuring of beliefs.

c. a return to some event during early childhood.

d. promoting an expression of feelings between members.

e. none of the above.

_____ 105. Which of the following is a typical procedure used in reality-therapy groups?

a. conducting an assessment of one's family constellation

b. exploring early childhood experiences

c. fostering transference reactions toward the leader

d. analyzing ego states

e. evaluating current behavior

_____ 106. Dreams are explored in

a. Gestalt groups.

b. psychoanalytic groups.

c. psychodrama groups.

d. Adlerian groups.

e. all of the above.

_____ 107. The object-relations theory is associated with

a. behavior therapy.

b. Gestalt therapy.

c. Adlerian therapy.

d. reality therapy.

e. none of the above.

_____ 108. Creativity and choice are stressed in

a. Adlerian therapy.

b. existential therapy.

c. reality therapy.

d. Gestalt therapy.

e. all of the above.

_____ 109. Insight is stressed in all of the approaches *except* for one.

a. psychoanalytic therapy

b. psychodrama

c. reality therapy

d. Gestalt therapy

e. TA

_____ 110. The process of skillful questioning would be used mostly by a group leader with which theoretical orientation?

a. person-centered therapy

b. reality therapy

c. Gestalt therapy

d. existential therapy

e. none of the above

_____ 111. Unfinished business and avoidance are key concepts of

a. Gestalt therapy.

b. reality therapy.

c. behavior therapy.

d. rational-emotive therapy.

e. none of the above.

_____ 112. Which type of group serves the function of re-creating the original family, so that members can work through their unresolved problems?

a. RET

b. behavioral

c. psychoanalytic

d. TA

e. person-centered

_____ 113. Individual psychology is another name for

a. psychoanalytic therapy.

b. Adlerian therapy.

c. existential therapy.

d. reality therapy.

e. person-centered therapy.

_____ 114. Contracts and homework assignments are most like to be used in

a. TA groups.

b. behavior-therapy groups.

c. reality-therapy groups.

d. RET groups.

e. all of the above.

_____ 115. Which approach would be least interested in the exploration of early childhood experiences?

a. reality therapy

b. psychoanalytic therapy

c. Gestalt therapy

d. Adlerian therapy

e. TA

_____ 116. A basic premise that we are not the victims of circumstances because we choose our behavior is emphasized in

a. existential therapy.

b. reality therapy.

c. person-centered therapy.

d. TA.

e. all of the above.

_____ 117. Concepts of introjection, projection, retroflection, confluence, and deflection are part of

a. Adlerian therapy.

b. psychodrama.

c. Gestalt therapy.

d. existential therapy.

e. TA.

_____ 118. The concept of basic psychological life positions is part of

a. psychoanalytic therapy.

b. TA.

c. psychodrama.

d. RET.

e. none of the above.

_____ 119. Which theory would be most concerned with understanding and exploring an individual's developmental stages?
   a. TA
   b. psychoanalytic therapy
   c. behavior therapy
   d. RET
   e. none of the above

_____ 120. The socioteleological approach that holds that people are primarily motivated by social forces and striving to achieve certain goals is
   a. person-centered therapy.
   b. existential therapy.
   c. reality therapy.
   d. Adlerian therapy.
   e. behavior therapy.

_____ 121. Which type of group counselor would tend to provide the least degree of direction?
   a. RET therapist
   b. person-centered therapist
   c. Gestalt therapist
   d. reality therapist
   e. behavior therapist

_____ 122. The here and now is emphasized in
   a. psychodrama.
   b. existential therapy.
   c. person-centered therapy.
   d. Gestalt therapy.
   e. all of the above.

_____ 123. Multimodal group therapy is associated with which theoretical approach?
   a. behavior therapy
   b. TA
   c. reality therapy
   d. Adlerian therapy
   e. existential therapy

_____ 124. The A-B-C theory is associated with
   a. reality therapy.
   b. TA.
   c. behavior therapy.
   d. RET.
   e. Gestalt therapy.

_____ 125. A focus on ego states would occur in
   a. Gestalt groups.
   b. Adlerian groups.
   c. TA groups.
   d. psychodrama groups.
   e. all of the above.

_____ 126. Which approach most relies on empirical research to validate its techniques?
   a. reality therapy
   b. behavior therapy
   c. person-centered therapy
   d. existential therapy
   e. TA

_____ 127. Cognitive homework is likely to be assigned in
   a. psychodrama groups.
   b. psychoanalytic groups.
   c. RET groups.
   d. reality-therapy groups.
   e. Gestalt groups.

_____ 128. Modeling would be important in which type of group?
   a. reality therapy
   b. behavior therapy
   c. RET
   d. existential therapy
   e. all of the above

_____ 129. Control theory is a basic part of the practice of
   a. behavior therapy.
   b. RET.
   c. reality therapy.
   d. Adlerian therapy.
   e. existential therapy.

_____ 130. The role of the family would be stressed mostly in which type of group?
   a. psychodrama
   b. behavioral
   c. existential
   d. Gestalt
   e. Adlerian

_____ 131. Injunctions, early decisions, and redecisions are key concepts stressed in which type of group?
   a. Adlerian
   b. TA
   c. Gestalt
   d. RET
   e. reality therapy

_____ 132. Which approach would be most likely to focus on an expression and exploration of feelings?
   a. behavioral therapy
   b. RET
   c. reality therapy
   d. Gestalt therapy
   e. none of the above

_____ 133. Significant developments in dealing with borderline and narcissistic personality disorders have occurred within which theory?
   a. Gestalt therapy
   b. TA
   c. behavior therapy
   d. person-centered therapy
   e. none of the above

_____ 134. Dealing with the present is stressed in
   a. psychodrama.
   b. Gestalt therapy.
   c. existential therapy.
   d. reality therapy.
   e. all of the above.

146

_____ 135. Which approach does not emphasize techniques?
   a. Adlerian therapy
   b. psychodrama
   c. existential therapy
   d. behavioral therapy
   e. RET

_____ 136. Which theory focuses on cognition?
   a. Adlerian
   b. Gestalt
   c. RET
   d. psychodrama
   e. two of the above

_____ 137. Success identity and positive addiction are basic concepts in
   a. TA.
   b. existential therapy.
   c. RET.
   d. reality therapy.
   e. Gestalt therapy.

_____ 138. A lifestyle investigation, which would focus on family background and would reveal a pattern of basic mistakes, would be used in
   a. psychoanalytic therapy.
   b. Adlerian therapy.
   c. behavioral therapy.
   d. RET.
   e. all of the above.

_____ 139. Which type of group leader is most likely to focus on energy and blocks to energy?
   a. Adlerian
   b. Gestalt
   c. psychoanalytic
   d. TA
   e. person-centered

_____ 140. The therapeutic conditions of congruence, unconditional positive regard, and empathy are emphasized in
   a. psychoanalytic therapy.
   b. reality therapy.
   c. TA.
   d. person-centered therapy.
   e. none of the above.

_____ 141. Role playing is likely to be used in
   a. psychodrama.
   b. Gestalt therapy.
   c. RET.
   d. behavioral therapy.
   e. all of the above.

_____ 142. The approach that stresses the total behavior of doing, thinking, feeling, and physiology is
   a. RET.
   b. reality therapy.
   c. person-centered therapy.
   d. psychoanalytic therapy.
   e. TA.

_____ 143. Which approach emphasizes the personal qualities of the group leader rather than the techniques of leading?
a. existential
b. person-centered
c. RET
d. behavioral
e. two of the above

_____ 144. The approach that teaches members how to identify irrational beliefs and substitute rational beliefs is
a. reality therapy.
b. RET.
c. TA.
d. Gestalt therapy.
e. behavioral therapy.

_____ 145. Social-skill-training groups most rely on which type of techniques?
a. behavioral
b. TA
c. psychodramatic
d. reality-therapy
e. Adlerian

_____ 146. In which type of group would members focus on their life scripts through the process of script analysis?
a. psychoanalytic
b. reality-therapy
c. behavioral
d. Adlerian
e. none of the above

_____ 147. Shame-attacking exercises are likely to be used in which type of group?
a. reality-therapy
b. person-centered
c. Gestalt
d. RET
e. psychodramatic

_____ 148. Which theoretical approach would most contribute to teaching members coping skills to manage stress?
a. person-centered therapy
b. reality therapy
c. Adlerian therapy
d. behavioral therapy
e. Gestalt therapy

_____ 149. The group leader assumes the role of a teacher in which approach?
a. TA
b. reality therapy
c. behavior therapy
d. RET
e. all of the above

_____ 150. Which approach has the goal of uncovering unconscious conflicts and working them through?
a. person-centered therapy
b. reality therapy

c. psychoanalytic therapy
d. TA
e. behavioral therapy

Essay Questions for Review and Study

Directions: These questions are designed as a study guide to help you pull together some central ideas in the textbook. Strive to write your answers briefly, using your own words.

1. What are the values of a group for special populations (children, adolescents, and adults)?

2. Differentiate between
   a. group psychotherapy and group counseling.
   b. group psychotherapy and self-help groups.

3. If you were working in a setting with clients representing diverse cultural backgrounds, what would you see as your major challenge as a group leader? How might you meet some of these challenges?

4. What do you see as a few of the advantages and disadvantages of group counseling with ethnic and minority clients?

5. What are some guidelines that could help you design and conduct groups with culturally diverse populations?

6. See Chapter 2 of this manual, and review the inventories that you filled out on ethical issues in group work. Have you changed your thinking from the beginning to the end of the course on any of these ethical issues?

7. Review the ASGW's ethical guidelines, and select one that you would most like to comment on.

8. Assume that you are a counselor in a community agency. No groups are being offered, and you see a need for several types of groups. What course of action, if any, might you be inclined to take?

9. When you think of conducting groups, what minimal training and preparation would you want?

10. Review the section in Chapter 3 that deals with the group leader as a person. What are your major personal characteristics that would help you and hinder you in your work as a group leader?

11. In the same chapter, review the section dealing with special problems and issues for beginning group leaders. Discuss your single most important concern.

12. Assume that you are working in an agency and would like to form a group. The director would like you to co-lead your groups. What specific things would you look for in selecting a co-leader?

13. Discuss what you see as your major tasks at each of the stages in the development of a group.

14. Assume that you are in a job interview and are asked this question: "Tell us about the theoretical orientation that guides your practice as a group counselor." How would you answer?

15. There are different styles of group leadership. Again, in a job interview, how might you describe your own personal style of leadership?

16. Think of a particular group that you might conduct, and describe briefly what factors you would consider in forming it.

17. The stages of a group do not generally flow neatly and predictably in the order described in the textbook. Why is it important that you have a clear understanding of the characteristics associated with the development of a group?

18. If you had to select the one theory that comes closest to your thinking and that helps you in your practice as a group counselor, which would it be? Explain the reasons for your selection.

19. Contrast a psychoanalytic group with a reality-therapy group in terms of goals and procedures used.

20. Dreams can be fruitfully explored by using several different therapy approaches. Show how you might work with a dream in a group format from these three perspectives: psychoanalytic, psychodrama, and Gestalt.

21. Compare the goals of psychodrama and Gestalt groups; contrast the differences in techniques between these two approaches.

22. Discuss some common denominators of these various approaches to group counseling: Adlerian therapy, TA, RET, reality therapy.

23. In what ways does reality therapy draw on both the existential and behavioral approaches?

24. Select one of the following possible combinations and discuss what you see as being some of the merits of merging the concepts and techniques of the two approaches as applied to group counseling: Gestalt with TA, Gestalt with RET, or Gestalt with reality therapy.

25. Assume that you are leading a group with culturally diverse members. Are there any concepts and techniques from the various approaches that you would find particularly useful?

26. Discuss some of the ways of combining existential themes with behavioral techniques. What are the possibilities of a merger between the existential and behavioral approaches as applied to group counseling?

27. What are some commonalities between a person-centered group and an existential group? What are some basic differences?

28. How would you describe your role as a group counselor to a new group? What do you see as your major leadership functions?

29. How would you assess the outcomes of a group that you were leading?

30. Discuss the role that theory plays in the practice of group counseling. How does the theory that one holds influence the interventions made by the leader?

Answer Key

1. c	2. d	3. a	4. d	5. b	6. e	7. b
8. a	9. c	10. e	11. b	12. c	13. e	14. b
15. e	16. b	17. b	18. e	19. c	20. e	21. c
22. b	23. a	24. c	25. b	26. a	27. b	28. e
29. a	30. b	31. F	32. T	33. T	34. F	35. T
36. F	37. T	38. T	39. T	40. F	41. F	42. F
43. T	44. F	45. F	46. F	47. T	48. T	49. F
50. F	51. b	52. e	53. c	54. a	55. a	56. d
57. b	58. e	59. b	60. d	61. c	62. c	63. c
64. a	65. a	66. b	67. d	68. c	69. d	70. a
71. b	72. a	73. e	74. b	75. d	76. c	77. b
78. e	79. a	80. d	81. c	82. e	83. e	84. a
85. a	86. a	87. b	88. c	89. d	90. c	91. c
92. b	93. b	94. c	95. b	96. e	97. e	98. a
99. e	100. b	101. c	102. a	103. e	104. b	105. e
106. e	107. e	108. e	109. c	110. b	111. a	112. c
113. b	114. e	115. a	116. e	117. c	118. b	119. b
120. d	121. b	122. e	123. a	124. d	125. c	126. b
127. c	128. e	129. c	130. e	131. b	132. d	133. e
134. e	135. c	136. e	137. d	138. b	139. b	140. d
141. e	142. b	143. e	144. b	145. a	146. e	147. d
148. d	149. e	150. c				

June 1, 1989 Final Draft

Approved by the Association for Specialists in Group Work (ASGW)

Executive Board, June 1, 1989

Ethical Guidelines for Group Counselors

Preamble

One characteristic of any professional group is the possession of a body of knowledge, skills, and voluntarily, self-professed standards for ethical practice. A Code of Ethics consists of those standards that have been formally and publicly acknowledged by the members of a profession to serve as the guidelines for professional conduct, discharge of duties, and the resolution of moral dilemmas. By this document, the Association for Specialists in Group Work (ASGW) has identified the standards of conduct appropriate for ethical behavior among its members.

The Association for Specialists in Group Work recognizes the basic commitment of its members to the Ethical Standards of its parent organization, the American Association for Counseling and Development (AACD) and nothing in this document shall be construed to supplant that code. These standards are intended to complement the AACD standards in the area of group work by clarifying the nature of ethical responsibility of the counselor in the group setting and by stimulating a greater concern for competent group leadership.

The group counselor is expected to be a professional agent and to take the processes of ethical responsibility seriously. ASGW views "ethical process" as being integral to group work and views group counselors as "ethical agents." Group counselors, by their very nature in being responsible and responsive to their group members, necessarily embrace a certain potential for ethical vulnerability. It is incumbent upon group counselors to give considerable attention to the intent and context of their actions because the attempts of counselors to influence human behavior through group work always have ethical implications.

The following ethical guidelines have been developed to encourage ethical behavior of group counselors. These guidelines are written for students and practitioners, and are meant to stimulate reflection, self-examination, and discussion of issues and practices. They address the group counselor's responsibility for providing information about group work to clients and the group counselor's responsibility for providing group counseling services to clients. A final section discusses the group counselor's responsibility for safeguarding ethical practice and procedures for reporting unethical behavior. Group counselors are expected to make known these standards to group members.

Ethical Guidelines

1. *Orientation and Providing Information*: Group counselors adequately prepare prospective or new group members by providing as much information about the existing or proposed group as necessary.

- Minimally, information related to each of the following areas should be provided.

    (a) Entrance procedures, time parameters of the group experience, group participation expectations, methods of payment (where appropriate), and termination procedures are explained by the group counselor as appropriate to the level of maturity of group members and the nature and purpose(s) of the group.

    (b) Group counselors have available for distribution, a professional disclosure statement that includes information on the group counselor's qualifications and group services that can be provided, particularly as related to the nature and purpose(s) of the specific group.

    (c) Group counselors communicate the role expectations, rights, and responsibilities of group members and group counselor(s).

(d) The group goals are stated as concisely as possible by the group counselor including "whose" goal it is (the group counselor's, the institution's, the parent's, the law's, society's, etc.) and the role of group members in influencing or determining the group's goal(s).

(e) Group counselors explore with group members the risks of potential life changes that may occur because of the group experience and help members explore their readiness to face these possibilities.

(f) Group members are informed by the group counselor of unusual or experimental procedures that might be expected in their group experience.

(g) Group counselors explain, as realistically as possible, what services can and cannot be provided within the particular group structure offered.

(h) Group counselors emphasize the need to promote full psychological functioning and presence among group members. They inquire from prospective group members whether they are using any kind of drug or medication that may affect functioning in the group. They do not permit any use of alcohol and/or illegal drugs during group sessions and they discourage the use of alcohol and/or drugs (legal or illegal) prior to group meetings which may affect the physical or emotional presence of the member or other group members.

(i) Group counselors inquire from prospective group members whether they have ever been a client in counseling or psychotherapy. If a prospective group member is already in a counseling relationship with another professional person, the group counselor advises the prospective group member to notify

the other professional of their participation in the group.

(j) Group counselors clearly inform group members about the policies pertaining to the group counselor's willingness to consult with them between group sessions.

(k) In establishing fees for group counseling services, group counselors consider the financial status and the locality of prospective group members. Group members are not charged fees for group sessions where the group counselor is not present and the policy of charging for sessions missed by a group member is clearly communicated. Fees for participating as a group member are contracted between group counselor and group member for a specified period of time. Group counselors do not increase fees for group counseling services until the existing contracted fee structure has expired. In the event that the established fee structure is inappropriate for a prospective member, group counselors assist in finding comparable services of acceptable cost.

2. *Screening of Members*: The group counselor screens prospective group members (when appropriate to their theoretical orientation). Insofar as possible, the counselor selects group members whose needs and goals are compatible with the goals of the group, who will not impede the group process, and whose well-being will not be jeopardized by the group experience. An orientation to the group (i.e., ASGW Ethical Guideline #1), is included during the screening process.

• Screening may be accomplished in one or more ways, such as the following:

(a) Individual interview,

(b) Group interview of prospective group members,

(c) Interview as part of a team staffing, and

(d) Completion of a written questionnaire by prospective group members.

3. *Confidentiality*: Group counselors protect members by defining clearly what confidentiality means, why it is important, and the difficulties involved in enforcement.

(a) Group counselors take steps to protect members by defining confidentiality and the limits of confidentiality (i.e., when a group member's condition indicates that there is clear and imminent danger to the member, others, or physical property, the group counselor takes reasonable personal action and/or informs responsible authorities).

(b) Group counselors stress the importance of confidentiality and set a norm of confidentiality regarding all group participants' disclosures. The importance of maintaining confidentiality is emphasized before the group begins and at various times in the group. The fact that confidentiality cannot be guaranteed is clearly stated.

(c) Members are made aware of the difficulties involved in enforcing and ensuring confidentiality in a group setting. The counselor provides examples of how confidentiality can non-maliciously be broken to increase members' awareness, and help to lessen the likelihood that this breach of confidence will occur. Group counselors inform group members about the potential consequences of intentionally breaching confidentiality.

(d) Group counselors can only ensure confidentiality on their part and not on the part of the members.

(e) Group counselors video or audio tape a group session only with the prior consent, and the members' knowledge of how the tape will be used.

(f) When working with minors, the group counselor specifies the limits of confidentiality.

(g) Participants in a mandatory group are made aware of any reporting procedures required of the group counselor.

(h) Group counselors store or dispose of group member records (written audio, video, etc.) in ways that maintain confidentiality.

(i) Instructors of group counseling courses maintain the anonymity of group members whenever discussing group counseling cases.

4. *Voluntary/Involuntary Participation*: Group counselors inform members whether participation is voluntary or involuntary.

(a) Group counselors take steps to ensure informed consent procedures in both voluntary and involuntary groups.

(b) When working with minors in a group, counselors are expected to follow the procedures specified by the institution in which they are practicing.

(c) With involuntary groups, every attempt is made to enlist the cooperation of the members and their continuance in the group on a voluntary basis.

(d) Group counselors do not certify that group treatment has been received by members who merely attend sessions, but did not meet the defined group expectations. Group members are informed about the consequences for failing to participate in a group.

5. *Leaving a Group*: Provisions are made to assist a group member to terminate in an effective way.

(a) Procedures to be followed for a group member who chooses to exit a group prematurely are discussed by the counselor with all group members either before the group begins, during a pre-screening interview, or during the initial group session.

(b) In the case of legally mandated group counseling, group counselors inform members of the possible consequences for premature self termination.

(c) Ideally, both the group counselor and the member can work cooperatively to determine the degree to which a group experience is productive or counterproductive for that individual.

(d) Members ultimately have a right to discontinue membership in the group, at a designated time, if the predetermined trial period proves to be unsatisfactory.

(e) Members have the right to exit a group, but it is important that they be made aware of the importance of informing the counselor and the group members prior to deciding to leave. The counselor discusses the possible risks of leaving the group prematurely with a member who is considering this option.

(f) Before leaving a group, the group counselor encourages members (if appropriate) to discuss their reasons for wanting to discontinue membership in the group. Counselors intervene if other members use undue pressure to force a member to remain in the group.

6. *Coercion and Pressure*: Group counselors protect member rights against physical threats, intimidation, coercion, and undue peer pressure insofar as is reasonably possible.

(a) It is essential to differentiate between "therapeutic pressure" that is part of any group and "undue pressure," which is not therapeutic.

(b) The purpose of a group is to help participants find their own answers, not to pressure them into doing what the group thinks is appropriate.

(c) Counselors exert care not to coerce participants to change in directions which they clearly state they do not choose.

(d) Counselors have responsibility to intervene when others use undue pressure or attempt to persuade members against their will.

(e) Counselors intervene when any member attempts to act out aggression in a physical way that might harm another member or themselves.

(f) Counselors intervene when a member is verbally abusive or inappropriately confrontive to another member.

7. *Imposing Counselor Values*: Group counselors develop an awareness of their own values and needs and the potential impact they have on the interventions likely to be made.

(a) Although group counselors take care to avoid imposing their values on members, it is appropriate that they expose their own beliefs, decisions, needs, and values, when concealing them would create problems for the members.

(b) There are values implicit in any group, and these are made clear to potential members before they join the group. (Examples of certain values include: expressing feelings, being direct and honest, sharing personal material with others, learning how to trust, improving interpersonal communication, and deciding for oneself.)

(c) Personal and professional needs of group counselors are not met at the members' expense.

(d) Group counselors avoid using the group for their own therapy.

(e) Group counselors are aware of their own values and assumptions and how these apply in a multicultural context.

(f) Group counselors take steps to increase their awareness of ways that their personal reactions to members might inhibit the group process and they monitor their countertransference. Through an awareness of the impact of stereotyping and discrimination (i.e., biases based on age, disability, ethnicity, gender, race, religion, or sexual preference), group counselors guard the individual rights and personal dignity of all group members.

8. *Equitable Treatment*: Group counselors make every reasonable effort to treat each member individually and equally.

(a) Group counselors recognize and respect differences (e.g., cultural, racial, religious, lifestyle, age, disability, gender) among group members.

(b) Group counselors maintain an awareness of their behavior toward individual group members and are alert to the potential detrimental effects of favoritism or partiality toward any particular group member to the exclusion or detriment of any other member(s). It is likely that group counselors will favor some members over others, yet all group members deserve to be treated equally.

(c) Group counselors ensure equitable use of group time for each member by inviting silent members to become involved, acknowledging nonverbal attempts to communicate, and discouraging rambling and monopolizing of time by members.

(d) If a large group is planned, counselors consider enlisting another qualified professional to serve as a co-leader for the group sessions.

9. *Dual Relationships*: Group counselors avoid dual relationships with group members that might impair their objectivity and professional judgment, as well as those which are likely to compromise a group member's ability to participate fully in the group.

(a) Group counselors do not misuse their professional role and power as group leader to advance personal or social contacts with members throughout the duration of the group.

(b) Group counselors do not use their professional relationship with group members to further their own interest either during the group or after the termination of the group.

(c) Sexual intimacies between group counselors and members are unethical.

(d) Group counselors do not barter (exchange) professional services with group members for services.

(e) Group counselors do not admit their own family members, relatives, employees, or personal friends as members to their groups.

(f) Group counselors discuss with group members the potential detrimental effects of group members engaging in intimate inter-member relationships outside of the group.

(g) Students who participate in a group as a partial course requirement for a group course are not evaluated for an academic grade based upon their degree of participation as a member in a group. Instructors of group counseling courses take steps to minimize the possible negative impact on students when they participate in a group course by separating course grades from participation in the group and by allowing students to decide what issues to explore and when to stop.

(h) It is inappropriate to solicit members from a class (or institutional affiliation) for one's private counseling or therapeutic groups.

10. *Use of Techniques*: Group counselors do not attempt any technique unless trained in its use or under supervision by a counselor familiar with the intervention.

(a) Group counselors are able to articulate a theoretical orientation that guides their practice, and they are able to provide a rationale for their interventions.

(b) Depending upon the type of an intervention, group counselors have training commensurate with the potential impact of a technique.

(c) Group counselors are aware of the necessity to modify their techniques to fit the unique needs of various cultural and ethnic groups.

(d) Group counselors assist members in translating in-group learnings to daily life.

11. *Goal Development*: Group counselors make every effort to assist members in developing their personal goals.

(a) Group counselors use their skills to assist members in making their goals specific so that others present in the group will understand the nature of the goals.

(b) Throughout the course of a group, group counselors assist members in assessing the degree to which personal goals are being met, and assist in revising any goals when it is appropriate.

(c) Group counselors help members clarify the degree to which the goals can be met within the context of a particular group.

12. *Consultation*: Group counselors develop and explain policies about between-session consultation to group members.

(a) Group counselors take care to make certain that members do not use between-session consultations to avoid dealing with issues pertaining to the group that would be dealt with best in the group.

(b) Group counselors urge members to bring the issues discussed during between-session consultations into the group if they pertain to the group.

(c) Group counselors seek out consultation and/or supervision regarding ethical concerns or when encountering difficulties which interfere with their effective functioning as group leaders.

(d) Group counselors seek appropriate professional assistance for their own personal problems or conflicts that are likely to impair their professional judgment and work performance.

(e) Group counselors discuss their group cases only for professional consultation and educational purposes.

(f) Group counselors inform members about policies regarding whether consultations will be held confidential.

13. *Termination from the Group*: Depending upon the purpose of participation in the group, counselors promote termination of members from the group in the most efficient period of time.

(a) Group counselors maintain a constant awareness of the progress made by each group member and periodically invite the group members to explore and reevaluate their experiences in the group. It is the responsibility of group counselors to help promote the independence of members from the group in a timely manner.

14. *Evaluation and Follow-up*: Group counselors make every attempt to engage in ongoing assessment and to design follow-up procedures for their groups.

(a) Group counselors recognize the importance of ongoing assessment of a group, and they assist members in evaluating their own progress.

(b) Group counselors conduct evaluation of the total group experience at the final meeting (or before termination), as well as ongoing evaluation.

(c) Group counselors monitor their own behavior and become aware of what they are modeling in the group.

(d) Follow-up procedures might take the form of personal contact, telephone contact, or written contact.

(e) Follow-up meetings might be with individuals, or groups, or both to determine the degree to which: (i) members have reached their goals, (ii) the group had a positive or negative effect on the participants, (iii) members could profit from some type of referral, and (iv) as information for possible modification of future groups. If there is no follow-up meeting, provisions are made available for individual follow-up meetings to any member who needs or requests such a contact.

15. *Referrals*: If the needs of a particular member cannot be met within the type of group being offered, the group counselor suggests other appropriate professional referrals.

(a) Group counselors are knowledgeable of local community resources for assisting group members regarding professional referrals.

(b) Group counselors help members seek further professional assistance, if needed.

16. *Professional Development*: Group counselors recognize that professional growth is a continuous, ongoing, developmental process throughout their career.

(a) Group counselors maintain and upgrade their knowledge and skill

competencies through educational activities, clinical experiences, and participation in professional development activities.

(b) Group counselors keep abreast of research findings and new developments as applied to groups.

Safeguarding Ethical Practice and Procedures for Reporting Unethical Behavior

The preceding remarks have been advanced as guidelines which are generally representative of ethical and professional group practice. They have not been proposed as rigidly defined prescriptions. However, practitioners who are thought to be grossly unresponsive to the ethical concerns addressed in this document may be subject to a review of their practices by the AACD Ethics Committee and ASGW peers.

- For consultation and/or questions regarding these ASGW Ethical Guidelines or group ethical dilemmas, you may contact the Chairperson of the ASGW Ethics Committee. The name, address, and telephone number of the current ASGW Ethics Committee Chairperson may be acquired by telephoning the AACD office in Alexandria, Virginia at (703) 823-9800.

- If a group counselor's behavior is suspected as being unethical, the following procedures are to be followed:

(a) Collect more information and investigate further to confirm the unethical practice as determined by the ASGW Ethical Guidelines.

(b) Confront the individual with the apparent violation of ethical guidelines for the purposes of protecting the safety of any clients and to help the group counselor correct any inappropriate behaviors. If satisfactory resolution is not reached through this contact then:

(c) A complaint should be made in writing, including the specific facts and dates of the alleged violation and all relevant supporting data. The complaint should be included in an envelope marked "CONFIDENTIAL" to ensure confidentiality for both the accuser(s) and the alleged violator(s) and forwarded to all of the following sources:

1. The name and address of the Chairperson of the state Counselor Licensure Board for the respective state, if in existence.

2. The Ethics Committee
   c/o The President
   American Association for Counseling and Development
   5999 Stevenson Avenue
   Alexandria, Virginia 22304

3. The name and address of all private credentialing agencies in which the alleged violator maintains credentials or holds professional membership. Some of these include the following:

   National Board for Certified Counselors, Inc.
   5999 Stevenson Avenue
   Alexandria, Virginia 22304

National Council for Credentialing of Career Counselors
c/o NBCC
5999 Stevenson Avenue
Alexandria, Virginia 22304

National Academy for Certified Clinical Mental Health Counselors
5999 Stevenson Avenue
Alexandria, Virginia 22304

Commission on Rehabilitation Counselor Certification
162 North State Street
Suite 317
Chicago, Illinois 60601

American Association for Marriage and Family Therapy
1717 K Street, N.W.
Suite 407
Washington, D. C. 20006

American Psychological Association
1200 Seventeenth Street, N.W.
Washington, D. C. 20036

American Group Psychotherapy Association, Inc.
25 East 21st Street, 6th Floor
New York, New York 10010

To the Owner of This Book

I hope that you have enjoyed the *Manual for Theory and Practice of Group Counseling* (third edition). I'd like to know as much about your experiences with the manual as possible. Only through your comments and the comments of others can I learn how to make the manual a better book for future readers.

School: _____ Your Instructor's Name: _____

1. What I like *most* about this manual is: _____

   _____

   _____

2. What I like *least* about this manual is: _____

   _____

   _____

3. My specific suggestions for improving the manual are: _____

   _____

4. Some ways in which I used this manual in class were: _____

   _____

   _____

5. Some ways in which I used this manual out of class were: _____

   _____

   _____

6. Some of the manual's exercises that were used most meaningfully in my class were: _____

   _____

7. My general reaction to this manual is: _____

8. In the space below or in a separate letter, please write any other comments about the book you'd like to make. I welcome your suggestions!

   _____

   _____

   _____

9. Please write down the name of the course in which you used this manual:

   _____

Optional:

Your Name: _____ Date: _____

May Brooks/Cole quote you, either in promotion for the *Manual for Theory and Practice of Group Counseling* or in future publishing ventures?

Yes _____ No _____

Sincerely,

Gerald Corey

FOLD HERE

NO POSTAGE
NECESSARY
IF MAILED
IN THE
UNITED STATES

BUSINESS REPLY MAIL
FIRST CLASS   PERMIT NO. 358   PACIFIC GROVE, CA

POSTAGE WILL BE PAID BY ADDRESSEE

ATT: Dr. Gerald Corey

Brooks/Cole Publishing Company
511 Forest Lodge Road
Pacific Grove, California 93950-9968

FOLD HERE